STUDY GUIDE

BOONE&KURTZBUSINESS

LOUIS E. BOONE

Ernest G. Cleverdon Chair of Business and Management
University of South Alabama

DAVID L. KURTZ

R.A. and Vivian Young Chair of Business Administration
University of Arkansas

DOUG COPELAND

Johnson County Community College

THE DRYDEN PRESS

HARCOURT BRACE COLLEGE PUBLISHERS

Fort Worth   Philadelphia   San Diego   New York   Orlando   Austin   San Antonio
Toronto   Montreal   London   Sydney   Tokyo

Address for Editorial Correspondence
The Dryden Press, 301 Commerce Street, Suite 3700, Fort Worth, TX 76102

Address for Orders
The Dryden Press, 6277 Sea Harbor Drive, Orlando, FL 32887
1-800-782-4479, or 1-800-433-0001 (in Florida)

ISBN: 0-03-016513-X

Printed in the United States of America

5 6 7 8 9 0 1 2 3 4   0 9 5   9 8 7 6 5 4 3 2 1

The Dryden Press
Harcourt Brace College Publishers

PREFACE

It has been my intention to create a *Study Guide* that *I would want as a student.* Therefore, this *Study Guide* has been designed to fulfill two major goals. First, by complementing the material presented in Louis E Boone's and David L Kurtz's BUSINESS I hope to increase your understanding and appreciation of business. If I am successful, you will be better equipped to respond intelligently to real-world issues that you read about and hear about every day. After all, many decisions made by business organizations have far-reaching implications for your personal life. Furthermore, a firm grasp of the principles of business is invaluable to those of you who are pursuing careers in business.

Second, and possibly of more immediate and practical concern to you, this *Study Guide* has been designed to prepare you for your examinations---to help you maximize your grade from this class given your limited studying time. I am confident that if you work through each chapter of the Workbook in its entirety after you have studied the chapter in the textbook, you will enter your tests with confidence and will score accordingly. I hope you come to view this *Study Guide* as a close and helpful companion---a much appreciated private tutor.

The format of each chapter begins with a list of the "Key Concepts" that are highlighted in the textbook. This can be found on one sheet of paper. This page, as well as all other pages, are perforated and can be easily removed from the book at your convenience.

The list of "Key Concepts" is followed by an "Analysis of Learning Goals" section which uses a variety of exercises designed to test your understanding of the material and to help you concentrate on what is important. The "Analysis of Learning Goals" exercises are chronologically organized to synchronize with the learning goals found in the textbook. Answers to this section, as well as all other sections, can be found at the end of each chapter in this *Study Guide*

The next section is a "Self Review" section which consists of True-False and Multiple Choice questions---the types of questions most of you will find on your exams. This is followed by an "Applications and Exercises" section designed to stimulate thought. To lighten thinks up a bit, a "Crossword Puzzle" rounds out the learning exercises.

The final section of each chapter provides the answers to all exercises and questions.

I have tried to be succinct, yet thorough enough for this *Study Guide* to be useful without it being "busy-work." I realize your time is valuable. But, I strongly encourage you to work through all of the exercises in this *Study Guide* in their entirety, after you have studied the textbook---including writing out your answers to the questions in the space provided when you are encouraged to do so (evidence shows that writing things out is a very effective way to assimilate and to learn material).

There is no doubt among educators that working through a study guide, like this one, proves to be time well spent! I hope you enjoy your course! Most of all, I hope you come to appreciate the study of business.

PEOPLE TO THANK

A very special thanks goes to Russ Boersma for recruiting me on this project and Lyn Hastert, editor, for allowing me to go forward. I also wish to thank Daryl Fox, also a Dryden editor, for his support and guidance. Finally, I wish to thank my wife, Mette, and my daughters Katrine and Nina for allowing me the time to complete this project.

Doug Copeland
Johnson County Community College

Contents

Chapter 1

Business: Blending People, Technology, and Ethical Behavior

"Today's business is unavoidably global in nature and quality products offering customer satisfaction are the result of blending technology, people, and ethical responsibility." (5)

KEY CONCEPTS

Business	All profit-seeking activities and enterprises that provide goods and services necessary to an economic system. (6)
Profits	Rewards for the businessperson who takes the risks involved in blending people, technology, and information in creating and marketing want-satisfying goods and services that provide customer satisfaction. (6)
Not-for-profit organizations	Firms whose primary objective is something other than returning profits to their owners. (6)
Private enterprise system	An economic system founded on the principle that competition among firms determines their success or failure in the marketplace and that this competition, in turn, best serves the needs of society. (Also known as capitalism.) (7)
Factors of production	Basic inputs into the private enterprise system, including natural resources, labor, capital, and entrepreneurship. (9)
Entrepreneurship	Taking risks to set up and operate a business. (10)
Productivity	The relationship between the number of units of goods and services produced and the number of inputs of human and other resources necessary to produce them. (10)
Gross domestic product (GDP)	The sum of all goods and services produced within a nation's boundaries. (11)

2

Pure competition	Many firms in an industry close enough in size that no single company can influence the prices charged in the marketplace. (11)
Monopolistic competition	Market situation where firms are able to differentiate their products from those of competitors. (12)
Oligopoly	Market in which there are few sellers. (12)
Monopoly	Market situation in which there are no competitors. (12)
Strategic alliances	Partnerships formed to create a competitive advantage. (13)
Technology	The application to business of knowledge based on discoveries in science, inventories, and innovations. (15)
Vision	The ability to perceive marketplace needs and what an organization must do to satisfy them. (20)
Critical thinking	The process of determining the authenticity, accuracy, and worth of information, knowledge claims, or arguments. (20)
Creativity	The development of novel solutions to perceived organizational problems. (20)
Diversity	The blend of persons of different genders, ethnic backgrounds, cultures, religions, ages, and physical and mental challenges. (22)
Business Ethics	The standard of business conduct and moral values. (22)
Social responsibility	A management philosophy that highlights the social and economic effects of managerial decisions. (22)

Name:_____ **Professor:**_____

Section:_____ **Date:**_____

ANALYSIS OF LEARNING GOALS

Learning Goal 1.1

Explain what a business is and how it operates within the private enterprise system.(5-7)

Multiple Choice:

1.   Business:
    a.   is an all-inclusive term that can be applied to many kinds of enterprises.
    b.   health and dynamism has little to do with the standard of living of a nation.
    c.   is the organization of people and technology for the production of goods but not services.
    d.   concepts discussed in the text do not apply to not-for-profit organizations.

2.   Business:
    a.   is the economic pulse of a nation and provides the means through which standards of living improve.
    b.   employs workers and produces goods and services for the satisfaction of consumers.
    c.   must satisfy customers if it wishes to make a profit.
    d.   all of the above.

3.   Profits:
    a.   equal total cost minus total revenue.
    b.   create an incentive for people to start a business in those markets where they are positive.
    c.   create an incentive for people to expand their businesses when they are negative.
    d.   are consistently rewarded to firms who do whatever is in their best short-term self-interest as opposed to doing what may be socially or ethically responsible.

4.   A major difference between a not-for-profit organization and a business is that a not-for profit organization does not have to:
    a.   secure sufficient revenues to remain in operation.
    b.   earn a profit for its owners.
    c.   develop objectives aimed at serving its constituency.
    d.   act socially and ethically responsible if it wishes to remain successful over time.

4

Learning Goal 1.2
Define the roles of competition and of the entrepreneur in a private enterprise system. (7-8)

True or False

_____1.   Once a firm has established a competitive edge in a market then it is assured continued success and loyalty from customers well into the future.

_____2.   Competition is destructive to an economy because it wastes too many resources producing low quality goods and services people don't really need and that's why antitrust laws have been passed.

_____3.   Anti-trust laws are designed to preserve the advantages of competition by prohibiting attempts to fix prices and monopolize markets.

_____4.   Competition exists only between profit-maximizing firms; the concept does not apply to workers, government, and not-for-profit organizations.

Learning Goal 1.3
Outline the basic rights of the free enterprise system. (8-9)

Multiple Choice

1.   The right of _____ is the most basic right under the free enterprise system.
   a.   private property.
   b.   profits.
   c.   freedom of choice.
   d.   competition.

2.   The private enterprise system also guarantees business owners the right to retain any after-tax earnings is the right to:
   a.   private property.
   b.   profits.
   c.   freedom of choice.
   d.   competition.

---

3.   The right to select a career, what you want to purchase, and where you wish to invest is
      the right to :
      a.   private property.
      b.   profits.
      c.   freedom of choice.
      d.   competition.

4.   Laws which prohibit price discrimination and deceptive advertising practices are included
      in the right of:
      a.   private property.
      b.   profits.
      c.   freedom of choice.
      d.   competition.

Learning Goal 1.4

Explain the concepts of gross domestic product and productivity. (10-11)

Matching

Match the following terms with the statements below.

a.   GDP
b.   Productivity
c.   Entrepreneurship
d.   Factors of production

_____1.   The relationship between the number of units of goods and services produced and
            the number of inputs of human and other resources necessary to produce them.

_____2.   Basic inputs into the private enterprise system, including natural resources, labor,
            capital, and entrepreneurship.

_____3.   The sum of all goods and services produced within a nation's borders.

_____4.   Taking risks to set up and operate a business.

6

Match the following factors of production with the income generated by their use.

_____5.   Natural resources   a.   Wages

_____6.   Labor   b.   Interest

_____7.   Capital   c.   Profits

_____8.   Entrepreneurship   d.   Rent

Learning Goal 1.5

Identify the degrees of competition that can exist in a private enterprise system. (11-12)

Fill in the Table

Characteristics:	Pure Competition	Monopolistic Competition	Oligopoly	Monopoly
Number of competitors				
Ease of entry into industry by new firms				
Similarity of product offered by competing firms				
Control over price by individual firms				
Real world example				

Learning Goal 1.6
Discuss the major challenges and opportunities facing managers in the late 1990s. (13-19)

Listing

List five challenges and opportunities facing managers in the late 1990s. They are the importance of:

_____ 1. Farming out one or more of a firm's in-house operations to a preferred vendor with a high-quality level of expertise in a particular task area.

_____ 2. Ironically, perhaps, the growing importance of technology makes it even more important for organizations to make effective use of this.

_____ 3. Partnerships formed to create a competitive advantage.

_____ 4. This is more difficult to measure in service industries than in manufacturing but it is essential that this be incorporated into the good or service produced to attract new customers and to keep current customers coming back.

_____ 5. The application to business of knowledge based on discoveries in science, inventions, and innovations.

Learning Goal 1.7
Discuss the most important qualities managers should possess. (19-22)

Listing

List five important qualities managers must possess if they wish to be successful.

_____ 1. They ability to manage change and to motivate others for the realization of a common goal.

8

_____2. The development of novel solutions to perceived organizational problems.

_____3. The ability to perceive marketplace needs and what an organization must do to satisfy them.

_____4. The process of determining the authenticity, accuracy, and worth of information, knowledge claims, or arguments.

_____5. Managing a blend of persons of different genders, ethnic backgrounds, cultures, religions, ages, and physical and mental challenges.

Learning Goal 1.8
Explain the ethical and social responsibilities of business. (22-23)

Fill in the blank

Most businesspeople believe in the principles of ethics and social responsibility.

_____ deals with the right and wrong actions that arise in any work

environment. _____ is a management philosophy that highlights the social

and economic effects of managerial decisions.

Name:_____ **Professor:**_____

Section:_____ **Date:**_____

SELF REVIEW
True or False

_____1.   Business includes all profit seeking activities and enterprises that provide goods and services necessary to an economic system.

_____2.   Profits create incentives for business people to undertake activities which improve the standard of living.

_____3.   Over time, profits are usually lower for firms who are socially responsible.

_____4.   Profits accrue to entrepreneurs and are a reward for their risk-taking.

_____5.   Businesses include not-for-profit organizations.

_____6.   Antitrust laws are generally accepted principles of business ethics and social responsibility.

_____7.   Competition is the battle among businesses for consumer acceptance.

_____8.   The right to profit means the right to get into any business one chooses.

_____9.   The barriers to entry entrepreneurs face when trying to enter a market to set up a business are greatest in an oligopoly market.

_____10.   The market environment which is characterized by the greatest amount of product differentiation is pure competition.

_____11.   If productivity rises then output, wages and the standard of living can rise.

_____12.   Partnerships formed to create a competitive advantage are called oligopolies.

_____13.   Technology results in new goods and services for consumers, better customer service, lower prices, and improved working conditions.

_____14.   Vision is an important managerial quality and it refers to the development of novel solutions to perceived organizational problems.

_____15.   Few businesses are committed to the principles of ethics and social responsibility.

Multiple Choice

1. Business enterprises:
   a. provide the bulk of employment and output produced in the United States.
   b. in today's world are unavoidably global in nature.
   c. in today's world must be concerned with producing a quality product.
   d. must be concerned with business ethics and social responsibility if they wish to be profitable over the long run.
   e. all of the above.

2. Profits:
   a. attract more entrepreneurs into a market resulting in more competition and therefore lower prices over time.
   b. are guaranteed for oligopolies.
   c. usually have little to do with how well the firm is satisfying customers.
   d. equal total costs plus total revenue.
   e. are earned by owners of capital.

3. Competition:
   a. is the battle among businesses for consumer acceptance.
   b. is so important that many states and federal laws have passed antitrust laws.
   c. is least prevalent in a monopoly market.
   d. requires firms to continually adjust their strategies, product offerings, service standards, and operating procedures.
   e. all of the above.

4. An entrepreneur:
   a. organizes, manages and directs the other factors of production in the production process.
   b. is a highly paid executive.
   c. is a highly paid worker.
   d. is a government employee.
   e. is a monopolist.

5. GDP:
   a. is the sum of all goods and services produced in the world.
   b. is the sum of all goods and services produced within a nation's boundaries.
   c. is the sum of all goods, but not services produced within a nation's boundaries.
   d. decreases when productivity rises.
   e. increases cause lower standards of living.

6. The private enterprise system grants all of the following rights *except*?
    a. The right of business owners to all profits after taxes.
    b. The freedom of choice right.
    c. The private property right.
    d. The right to be fully employed.
    e. The right of citizens to establish the rules of competition.

7. Monopolistic competition is characterized by:
    a. a few dominant sellers in the market.
    b. government regulation of the entry of new businesses into the market.
    c. firms differentiating their good or service from each other.
    d. firms having no control over their price.
    e. all of the above.

8. Which of the following markets has the greatest ease of entry by new competitors?
    a. International market.
    b. Pure competition
    c. Monopoly.
    d. Monopolistic competition.
    e. Oligoply.

9. Partnerships between firms formed to create a competitive advantage is an example of businesses facing the challenge of:
    a. increasing quality.
    b. reducing costs through outsourcing.
    c. investing in their work force.
    d. creating strategic alliances.
    e. improving technology.

10. Business ethics and social responsibility:
    a. sounds good, but in practice it usually just increases a firm's costs and reduces profits over time.
    b. has little support in the business community.
    c. requires very little flexibility on the part of management.
    d. includes addressing the needs of the public and workers.
    e. rarely entails dilemmas for management.

Name:_____Professor:_____
Section:_____Date:_____

APPLICATION EXERCISES

1. What positive role can government play in perpetuating business? How can government hurt business?

2. Assume you are the owner of a firm in an oligopoly. One of your competitors has just increased her price. What should you do? Increase or decrease your price? Why? What if your competitor decreased her price?

14

3.   You are at a party and people are discussing the changing role of American business in the international global marketplace---great party! Someone comments that it seems as though American business is "all washed out"----America just can't compete anymore. As a student in a business course they ask you what American business needs to do to increase its competitiveness in the new global market place. How do you respond?

Name:_____ **Professor:**_____

Section:_____ **Date:**_____

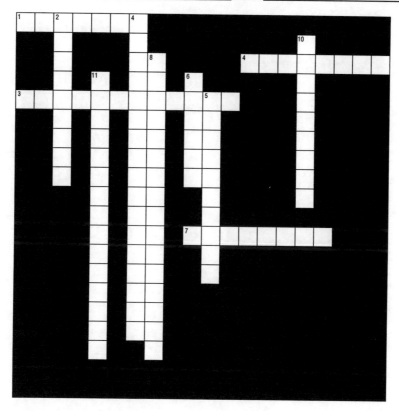

ACROSS

1. Rewards for the businessperson who takes the risks involved in blending people, technology, and information in creating and marketing want-satisfying goods and services that provide customer satisfaction.

3. The relationship between the number of units of goods and services produced and the number of inputs of human and other resources necessary to produce them.

7. Market situation in which there are no competitors.

9. All profit-seeking activities and enterprises that provide goods and services necessary to an economic system.

DOWN

2. Market in which there are few sellers.

4. Partnership formed to create a competitive advantage. (2 words)

5. The application to business of knowledge based on discoveries in science, inventories, and innovations.

6. The ability to perceive marketplace needs and what an organization must do to satisfy them.

8. The process of determining the authenticity, accuracy, and worth of information, knowledge claims, or arguments. (2 words)

10. The blend of persons of different genders, ethnic backgrounds, cultures, religions, ages, and physical and mental challenges.

11. Many firms in an industry close enough in size that no single company can influence the prices charged in the marketplace. (2 words)

CHAPTER 1 SOLUTIONS
Analysis of Learning Goals

Learning Goal 1.1

1. a   2. d   3. b   4. b

Learning Goal 1.2

1. False   2. False   3. True   4. False

Learning Goal 1.3

1. a   2. b   3. c   4. d

Learning Goal 1.4

1. b   5. d
2. d   6. a
3. a   7. b
4. c   8. c

Learning Goal 1.5

Characteristics:	Pure Competition	Monopolistic Competition	Oligopoly	Monopoly
Number of competitors	Many	Few to many	Few	No direct competitors
Ease of entry into industry by new firms	Easy	Somewhat difficult	Difficult	Regulated by government
Similarity of product offered by competing firms	Similar	Different	Can be similar to different	No directly competing goods and services
Control over price by individual firms	None	Some	Some	Considerable in a pure monopoly; little in a regulated monopoly
Real world example	A farmer	A retail store	A steel producer	Local electric company

18

Learning Goal 1.6
1.　Outsourcing
2.　Human resources (people)
3.　Strategic alliances
4.　Quality
5.　Technology

Learning Goal 1.7
1.　Leadership
2.　Creativity
3.　Vision
4.　Critical thinking
5.　Diversity

Learning Goal 1.8
Business ethics
Social responsibility

Self-Review

True or False
1. T	4. T	7. T	10. F	13. T
2. T	5. F	8. F	11. T	14. F
3. F	6. F	9. F	12. F	15. F

Multiple Choice
1. e	4. a	7. c	10. d
2. a	5. b	8. b	
3. e	6. d	9. d	

Application Exercises

1.　Government can play a positive role in perpetuating business by creating a legal and political environment which is conducive to business and in ensuring an adequate infrastructure.

　　A legal environment conducive to business means the government protects the basic rights of the free enterprise system---private property, the right to profits, freedom of choice, and establishing rules of the game (antitrust laws) which perpetuate competition. A political environment conducive to business means keeping business taxes and regulations reasonable so as to not too adversely effect the incentive for entrepreneurs to invest in businesses. An adequate infrastructure entails providing for acceptable roads, etc... (and this requires tax revenues).

Government can hurt business by reducing incentives to invest with unreasonably high taxes, over-zealous enforcement of antitrust and other forms of regulation ostensibly designed to promote competition but in practice actually act as a barrier to entry for firms (thereby inhibiting competition in a market). Warning: be careful to come to quick conclusions concerning whether a particular government action helps or hurts. It probably does both---its just a matter of whether the benefits to society outweigh the costs. That's for you to decide after considerable investigation and thought.

2. If your competitor increased her price you should not. By not increasing your price you would be able to take away many of her customers, thereby increasing your profits. If your competitor decreased her price you would be forced to do the same to preserve your market share of the industry's total sales. Now that you and your competitor, as well as the other few firms in the oligopoly, are all selling at lower prices, then you will all be worse off. These type of "price wars" are mutually destructive. This is why one typically observes prices in an oligopoly as being rather "sticky" (they don't change by much very often).

3. First, American business is not "all washed out." However, there are some real challenges that face American business in the latter 1990s. These include forming strategic alliances to create a competitive advantage, a firm commitment to producing the highest quality product possible, utilizing the latest technology, a firm commitment to effective use of human resources, and using outsourcing to reduce costs and to increase competitiveness.

Crossword Puzzle

CHAPTER 1

Chapter 2

Business: Its Environment and Role in Society

"There are five major environmental factors that impact business: competition, regulation, the economy, the social/cultural environment, and technology." (30)

KEY CONCEPTS

Research and development (R&D)	The scientific process of developing new commercial products. (31)
Customer service	The aspects of competitive strategy that refers to how a firm treats its customers. (31)
Regulated industry	One in which competition is either limited or eliminated, and government monitoring substitutes for the market controls. (33)
Deregulation	The movement toward eliminating legal restraints on competition in various industries. (33)
Economics	The social science of allocating scarce resources and is the study of people and their behavior. (36)
Supply	Refers to sellers' willingness and ability to provide goods and services for sale in a market. (36)
Demand	Refers to buyers' willingness and ability to purchase goods and services. (36)

22

Ecology	The study of the relationship between living things and their environment. (40)
Pollution	Tainting or destroying a natural environment. (40)
Recycling	Reprocessing used material so they can be reused. (41)
Conservation	Preserving our declining energy resources. (41)
Consumerism	The public demand for business to consider consumer wants and needs in making its decisions. (42)
Family leave	Giving employees a leave of absence from work in order to deal with family matters. (43)
Equal Employment Opportunity Commission (EEOC)	Was created to increase job opportunities for women and minorities and to help end job discrimination based on race, color, religion, sex, or national origin in any personnel action. (43)
Affirmative action program	To increase job opportunities for women, minorities, the disabled, and other protected categories. (43)
Multicultural diversity	The racial and cultural blend within a society. (43)
Sexual harassment	Inappropriate actions of a sexual nature. (43)
Sexism	Discrimination against either sex, but it primarily occurs against women. (44)

Name:_____ **Professor:**_____

Section:_____ **Date:**_____

ANALYSIS OF LEARNING GOALS

Learning Goal 2.1 (31-33)
Discuss the competitive issues that the United States faces in an increasingly global economy.

Listing

List four competitive issues in an increasingly global issue. They are:

_____1.   The scientific process of developing new commercial products.

_____2.   The aspect of competitive strategy that refers to how a firm treats its customers.

_____3.   This will enable people to ask questions, define problems, combine information form many different sources, and deal with topics that stretch across disciplines and cultures.

_____4.   This will enable companies to move fast---to adjust, to correct more quickly.

Learning Goal 2.2
Explain how government regulates business. (33-35)

---

1.   Government regulates competition and competitors as well as specific business practices. Government control takes two broad forms. What are they?

24

2.   What is deregulation? Briefly describe the impact it can have on business.

3.   Study pages 34 and 35. They list some laws pertaining to competition and various commercial practices. You may see some exam questions related to these.

Learning Goal 2.3
Summarize the relationship between supply, demand and price. (36)

Multiple Choice

1.   Economics:
      a.   is the study of the allocation of scarce resources among unlimited wants.
      b.   the study of the relationship between living things and their environment.
      c.   seeks to understand the choices consumers make but not the choices businesses make.
      d.   is concerned with the domestic economy, not international trade.

2.   Microeconomics is concerned with:
      a.   unemployment levels in the national economy.
      b.   policies designed to improve a nation's standard of living.
      c.   inflation rates in the national economy.
      d.   some particular segment of the economy.

3.   The demand curve:
      a.   shows how much producers will produce and make available in the market at various prices.
      b.   shows that as the price rises producers will produce and make available in the market a greater quantity.
      c.   shows how much buyers are willing and able to purchase at various prices.
      d.   shows that as the price rises buyers are willing and able to purchase a greater amount.

---

4.   According to the laws of supply and demand, if:
    a.   the price in a market is above equilibrium then the quantity supplied exceeds the quantity demanded and a surplus will be observed.
    b.   the price in a market is below equilibrium then the quantity demanded exceeds the quantity supplied and a shortage will be observed.
    c.   a surplus exits in a market then the price will fall; whereas if a shortage exists, the price will rise.
    d.   all of the above.

Learning Goal 2.4
Describe how the social-cultural environment can impact business. (37)

---

1.   Describe some of the trends which exist in our society and culture which affect business decisions?

2.   Why is the social-cultural context for business decision making more pronounced in the international sphere than in the domestic arena?

Learning Goal 2.5
Discuss ways in which the technological environment can affect business. (37-38)

True or False

_____1.   New technology results in new goods and services as well as the improvement of existing products.

_____2.   New technology often lowers the price of products through the development of more cost-effective production and distribution techniques.

_____3.   Technology cannot make existing products obsolete.

_____4.   Increases in technology have never spawned the development of entirely new industries.

Learning Goal 2.6
Outline business's responsibilities to the general public. (38-41)

Fill in the Blank

Responsibilities of business to the general public include dealing with _____,

which includes dealing with smoking, secondhand smoke, alcohol and substance abuse, and

educating employees about AIDS. _____ means reducing the impact of

business on the environment (working to minimize pollution, acid rain, and the greenhouse

effect; supporting recycling; and conserving and developing our energy resources). Additionally,

it is important to business to develop _____, since a well-educated, skilled

work force is a nation's most valuable asset.

Matching

Match the following terms with their definitions.

_____1.   Ecology   a.   Preserving our declining energy resources.

_____2.   Pollution   b.   Reprocessing used material so they can be reused.

_____3.   Recycling   c.   Tainting or destroying a natural environment.

_____4.   Conservation   d.   The study of the relationship between living things
                                         and their environment.

Learning Goal 2.7
Identify business's responsibilities to customers. (42)

True or False

_____1.   Consumerism is not a major social and economic movement.

_____2.   Consumerism is the public demand for business to consider consumer wants and
           needs in making its decisions.

_____3.   Consumerism has had the net effect of passing numerous consumer protection
           laws.

_____4.   President Kennedy outlined the consumer's rights as the right to be safe, informed,
           to choose, and to be heard.

Learning Goal 2.8
Describe business's responsibilities to employees. (42-44)

Listing

List the 5 responsibilities businesses have to employees. They pertain to:

_____1.   Giving employees a leave of absence from work in order to deal
                            with family matters.

_____ 2. Was created to increase job opportunities for women and minorities and to help end job discrimination based on race, color, religion, sex, or national origin in any personnel action.

_____ 3. To increase job opportunities for women, minorities, the disabled, and other protected categories.

_____ 4. The racial and cultural blend within a society.

_____ 5. Inappropriate actions of a sexual nature.

Learning Goal 2.9

Explain business's responsibilities to investors and to the financial community. (44-45)

---

1. Explain why *both* legal and ethical business practices in the financial community is so important.

Name:_____ **Professor:**_____

Section:_____ **Date:**_____

SELF REVIEW

True or False

_____1. The skills that are demanded in the U.S. work force are changing rapidly, requiring workers to adopt a philosophy of life-long learning.

_____2. Customer service is defined as the scientific process of developing new commercial products.

_____3. Public utilities are examples of government regulated monopolies.

_____4. The Sherman Antitrust Act is one of the most recent laws aimed at maintaining a competitive environment.

_____5. Microeconomics is concerned with a particular segment of the economy.

_____6. The equilibrium price exists at the point of intersection between the demand and supply curves.

_____7. Business strategies that work in the United States often cannot be applied directly in other countries.

_____8. Technology is important to engineers but is rarely relevant for marketing managers interested in increasing sales.

_____9. Acting socially and ethically irresponsible can cause a firm to go out of business.

_____10. Business should not do anything about increasing the quality of the work force because that is the responsibility of each individual worker.

_____11. The recycling of all containers is both possible and profitable.

_____12. The net effect of consumerism has been the passage of numerous laws protecting businesses from the abuses of consumer boycotts and slander campaigns.

_____13. Developing a better understanding of people's cultures and behaviors will help business people manage culturally diverse staffs more effectively.

_____14. There is probably no place the public expects a higher level of business ethics than in the arena of financial transactions.

Multiple Choice

1. A firm's competitiveness:
    a. used to primarily depend on keeping its costs down, and using resources in close geographic proximity of the company's facilities.
    b. now depends on product design.
    c. now depends on product development.
    d. now depends on the efficient use of technology.
    e. all of the above.

2. Government regulation of business:
    a. consists only of the enactment of statutes affecting competition and various commercial practices.
    b. takes the form of direct regulation of business to promote the public interest and the enactment of statutes affecting competition and various commercial practices.
    c. consists only of the direct regulation of public utilities.
    d. always results in an increase in the quality of goods and services provided to the public.
    e. is never appropriate.

3. Which of the following statements is true?
    a. The Sherman Antitrust Act of 1890 prohibits restraint of trade and monopolization.
    b. The Federal Trade Commission Act prohibits unfair methods of competition and established the Federal Trade Commission.
    c. The North American Free Trade Agreement (NAFTA) is an international agreement between Canada, Mexico, and the United States that facilitates trade by removing tariffs and other trade barriers among the three nations.
    d. The Family and Medical Leave Act requires covered employers to grant up to 12 weeks of unpaid job protected leave to eligible employees.
    e. All of the above.

4. According to economic analysis of a market:
    a. at the equilibrium price the quantity demanded equals the quantity supplied.
    b. the demand side of the market is looking from the sellers' perspective and indicates that as the price goes up sellers will supply more.
    c. the supply side of the market is looking from the buyers' perspective and indicates that as the price goes up buyers will buy less.
    d. surpluses cause prices to rise; shortages cause prices to fall.
    e. if the price is above equilibrium a shortage will be observed in the market; if the price is below equilibrium a surplus will be observed.

5.   In economic analysis, supply:
   a.   refers to sellers' willingness and ability to provide goods and services for sale in a market.
   b.   refers to buyers' willingness and ability to purchase goods and services.
   c.   is represented by a curve which slopes downward.
   d.   will increase if price falls.
   e.   and demand determines the amount bought and sold, but not the price.

6.   The social-cultural context for business decision making suggests that:
   a.   successful marketing strategies in the United States, because we are so culturally diverse, will be successful in other countries.
   b.   all businesses should focus on the broader market and not pay attention to specific sub-markets.
   c.   consumers are going to have to adjust their consumption habits to the kinds of goods and services businesses will be offering in the future.
   d.   businesses are going to have to adjust to the changing values and demographics of consumers if they wish to be successful in the future.
   e.   learning about culture and societal differences among countries is a waste of time and money.

7.   Business' role in protecting the environment to meet the responsibilities it has to the general public means:
   a.   providing family and medical leave for employees.
   b.   proving on-the-job training for workers.
   c.   testing employees for AIDS.
   d.   ensuring that employees are not sexually harassed on the job.
   e.   taking steps to reduce environmental pollution.

8.   Which of the following is one of the consumer rights advocated by President Kennedy?
   a.   The right of the public to vote on who runs a company.
   b.   The right of consumers to have as much of a product as they need.
   c.   The right of consumers to have safe products.
   d.   The right of consumers to live in a pollution-free environment.
   e.   The right of consumers to a fair price.

9.   The Civil Rights Act of 1964 established:
   a.   discrimination in the work force.
   b.   the Equal Employment Opportunity Commission.
   c.   multicultural diversity in the labor force.
   d.   sexism in the job place.
   e.   comparable pay for comparable work.

32

10.	Which of the following statements is true regarding business responsibility to investors and the financial community?
	a.	In the last several years there has been little publicity concerning these affairs.
	b.	The public expects this behavior to be *both* legal and ethical.
	c.	It is commonplace for government regulatory officials to receive bribes.
	d.	Few people are hurt if businesses undertake unethical stock and bond trading.
	e.	all of the above.

Name:_____ **Professor:**_____
Section:_____ **Date:**_____

APPLICATION EXERCISES

1.   a.   Why is it so important for top management to make a firm commitment to ethically and socially responsible behavior on the part of the company if it is to be successful?

        b.   What are some suggestions for achieving an ethically corporate culture which could help give rise to more socially responsible behavior on the part of business?

34

2.   There have been reports of an automobile manufacturer who was aware that the placement of the gas tank in the location chosen could give rise to the vehicle exploding on impact from a certain angle. Assuming those reports are true, is that ethically and socially responsible behavior on the part of that manufacturer? What could have motivated the manufacturer to continue to produce and sell this vehicle even though they may have knowledge of its problems?

3.   Is it ethical for a firm to make exaggerated claims about its product, even when it is willing to back those claims up with a "money back" guarantee, when it realizes that few customers will go to the trouble of getting their money back possibly because the company has made it so difficult? Consider a case where consumers may not have been aware that in order to get their money back they are required to fill out, stamp (at their expense) and return within 30 days of the purchase one of those little note cards which may, or may not have been found in the package.

Name:_____ Professor:_____

Section:_____ Date:_____

CROSSWORD PUZZLE

ACROSS

1. An industry in which competition is either limited or eliminated, and government monitoring substitutes for the market controls. (2 words)

3. The social science of allocating scarce resources and is the study of people and their behavior.

6. Giving employees a leave of absence from work in order to deal with family matters. (2 words)

7. Preserving our declining energy resources.

9. Tainting or destroying a natural environment.

10. Refers to buyers' willingness and ability to purchase goods and services.

DOWN

2. The aspects of competitive strategy that refers to how a firm treats its customers. (2 words)

4. The study of the relationship between living things and their environment.

5. Reprocessing used material so they can be reused.

8. Discrimination against either sex, but it primarily occurs against women.

CHAPTER 2 SOLUTIONS

Analysis of Learning Goals

Learning Goal 2.1
1.   Researching and developing better products.
2.   Customer service
3.   Improving the competitiveness of the work force
4.   Improving organizational flexibility

Learning Goal 2.2
1.   Government control takes two broad forms: (a) the regulation of industry (the type of regulation in which competition is either limited or eliminated and government monitoring substitutes for the market controls---e.g. public utilities are regulated); and (b) the enactment of statutes (state and federal laws affecting competition and various commercial practices).

2.   Deregulation is the movement toward eliminating legal restraints on competition in various industries. It can either increase or decrease competition depending on the circumstances unique to each case.

Learning Goal 2.3
1. a   2. d   3. c   4. d

Learning Goal 2.4
1.   There is a consumer trend toward placing increased value on convenience and speed. Our population is getting older and there are opportunities for business to respond to the unique demands of sub-markets which exist in our culturally diverse society. Businesses which adapt to changing social and cultural trends will enhance their success.

2.   Cultural and societal differences are more pronounced among countries than within a given country. Therefore, businesses need to be knowledgeable of other society's and their values, and remember to remain flexible---what "works" in one country may not in another.

Learning Goal 2.5
1. True   2. True   3. False   4. False

Learning Goal 2.6
public health issues
protecting the environment
a quality work force

38

1. d   2. c   3. b   4. a

Learning Goal 2.7
1. False   2. True   3. True   4. True

Learning Goal 2.8
1.   Family Leave
2.   Equal Employment Opportunity Commission (EEOC)
3.   Affirmative Action Program
4.   Multicultural diversity
5.   Sexual harassment

Learning Goal 2.9
1.   When business does not meet its social responsibility in this area then hundreds, if not thousands, of people can suffer---they can lose not only their investments, but some people could lose their jobs.

Self-Review
True or False
1. T	4. F	7. T	10. F	13. T
2. F	5. T	8. F	11. F	14. T
3. T	6. T	9. T	12. F	

Multiple Choice
1. e	4. a	7. e	10. b
2. b	5. a	8. c	
3. e	6. d	9. b	

Application Exercises

1.   a.   Top management must make a firm commitment to social responsibility and ethical business practices if it is to be successful because then employees will know it is a top priority for the firm.

       b.   Suggestions for achieving an ethical corporate culture include:
              1.   Develop a written code of ethics.
              2.   Make the code as specific to the company as possible.
              3.   Establish an anonymous reporting procedure for internal problem solving.
              4.   Involve all employees in identifying ethical issues.
              5.   Include ethical decision making in employee's performance appraisals.
              6.   Publicize executive priorities and efforts related to social issues.

2. This type of behavior would be determined unethical and socially irresponsible by most people. It may have been undertaken because the estimated cost of fixing the design, or recalling the vehicle, may have been greater than the injury or death settlements in or out of court.

3. There is no "right" or "wrong" answer. This is an issue you must decide.

Crossword Puzzle

CHAPTER 2

Chapter 3

Global and Economic Forces Affecting Business

"We can divide international business into three major activities: exporting, importing, and foreign production." (51)

KEY CONCEPTS

Exporting	Selling domestic goods and services abroad. (51)
Importing	Purchasing foreign goods, raw materials, and services. (51)
Foreign production	Making goods and supplying services in a foreign country for sale there or in other countries. (51)
Communism	All property would be shared by the people of a community. (51)
Socialism	The government owns and operates key industries. Private ownership is allowed for industries that are considered less crucial. (53)
Mixed economy	An economy with a combination of government ownership and private ownership. (53)
Privatization	Converting government-owned companies into privately held firms. (53)
Balance of trade	The relationship between a nation's exports and imports. (54)
Balance of Payments	The overall flow of money into and out of a country. (54)
Exchange rate	The rate at which a country's currency can be exchanged for the currencies of other nations. (54)

Devaluation	The fall of a currency's value relative to other currencies or to a fixed standard. (55)
Countertrade	An international agreement in which an exporter must buy something in order to sell something else. (58)
Joint venture	When a firm enters into a foreign market with a local firm or government, sharing the operation's costs, risks, management, and profits with its local partner. (58)
Multinational corporation	A firm with major operations outside its home country. (58)
Tariff	A tax levied on products imported from abroad. (59)
Quota	A limit on the number of certain products that can be imported. (59)
Embargo	A total ban on imported or exported products. (59)
General Agreement of Tariffs and Trade (GATT)	An international trade accord that has sponsored a series of negotiations that have reduced worldwide tariff levels. (61)
Dumping	Selling goods abroad at a price lower than that charged in the domestic market. Is prohibited in many countries. (62)
Free trade area	Participating nations trade freely among themselves without tariffs or trade restrictions. (62)
Customs union	Sets up a free trade area, plus a uniform tariff for trade with nonmember nations. (63)
Common Market	Members go beyond a customs union to try to bring all government trade rules into agreement. (63)
Global strategy	A business strategy which uses a standardized product and marketing strategy worldwide. (64)
Multinational strategy	A business strategy in which each national market is treated differently. (65)

Name:_____ **Professor:**_____
Section:_____**Date:**_____

ANALYSIS OF LEARNING GOALS

Learning Goal 3.1
Explain the importance of international business. (50-51)

1.   Why must U.S. businesses concern themselves with international trade?

2.   Write out the term described by each of the following definitions.

   a. _Exporting_ is the selling of domestic goods and services abroad.

   b. _Foreign Production_ is making goods and supplying services in a foreign country for sale there or in another country.

   c. _Importing_ is the purchase of foreign goods, raw materials, and services.

Learning Goal 3.2
Identify the different types of economic systems. (51-54)

Multiple choice

1.   Communism is an economic system:
   a.   in which the government owns the means of production with few exceptions, like small tracts of land.
   b.   in which the government owns and operates key industries, but private ownership is allowed for industries that are considered less crucial.
   c.   in which there is a combination of government ownership and private ownership.
   d.   which has been very successful in providing for a high standard of living for its people.

44

2.	Karl Marx is often quoted as having said:
	a.	"ask not what your country can do for you, ask what you can do for your country."
	b.	"it's best to remain silent and thought a fool than to speak up and remove all doubt."
	c.	"from each according to his ability, to each according to his needs."
	d.	to be or not to be."

3.	The republics of the former Soviet Union:
	a.	have been adopting western style market-driven economic systems.
	b.	have been involved in converting their factories from defense-oriented production to consumer goods.
	c.	have opened up their economies to new business opportunities for Westerners.
	d.	all of the above.

4.	Which of the following statements is true?
	a.	Most real-world economies are mixed economies.
	b.	Privatization is the act of converting government-owned companies into privately held firms.
	c.	An objective of privatization is often to increase the efficiency of a formerly government-run industry.
	d.	all of the above.

Learning Goal 3.3

Discuss the economic concepts involved in international business. (54-55)

Matching

Match the following terms with the statements below.

a.	Balance of trade
b.	Trade surplus
c.	Trade deficit
d.	Balance of payments

e.	Balance of payments surplus
f.	Balance of payments deficit
g.	Exchange rate
h.	Devaluation

___E___ 1.	When more money is coming into a country from abroad than is leaving it.

___D___ 2.	The overall flow of money into or out of a country.

A 3.   The relationship between a country's exports and imports.

B 4.   When a country exports more than it imports.

G 5.   The rate at which a nation's currency can be exchanged for the currencies of other nations.

H 6.   The fall of a currency's value relative to other currencies or to a fixed standard.

F 7.   When more money is leaving a country than entering it.

C 8.   When a country imports more than it exports.

Learning Goal 3.4

Explain why nations tend to specialize in certain goods. (56-57)

True or False

T 1.   Specialization and trade along the lines of comparative advantage is mutually beneficial for all economies involved.

T 2.   Absolute advantage in the production of a product means the product can be produced at the lowest cost.

T 3.   A country has a comparative advantage in the production of an item if it can supply that item more efficiently and at a lower cost than it can supply other goods, compared to other nations.

F 4.   A country should specialize in the production of the good for which it has an absolute advantage.

46

Learning Goal 3.5
Name the different levels of involvement in international business. (57-58)

Listing

List the different types of involvement in international business.

Indirect Exporting When a firm's product is part of another good that is exported.

Direct Exporting 2. When a firm actually seeks export business.

Foreign Licensing A contact in which a firm allows a foreign company to produce and distribute its products or use its trademarks, patents, or process in a specific geographic area.

Overseas Marketing 4. When a firm establishes a foreign sales office.

Combined 5. When a company produces as well as markets it products abroad.
Foreign Production and Marketing

Learning Goal 3.6
Explain countertrade. (58)

---

1.   What is countertrade?

2.   What is a multinational corporation?

Learning Goal 3.7
Identify the main obstacles confronting global business. (58-62)

Fill in the Blank

Various barriers to international business exist. Differences in language, education, social values, religious attitudes, and consumer habits create _cutural barriers_ barriers. Geographic considerations and different time zones between nations create _physical barriers_ barriers. A tax levied on products imported from abroad are called _tariff_ and they too can effect global commerce. In addition, there are also _import quota_ which set a limit on the number on certain products that can be imported into a country. A final type of trade barrier, which is a total ban on an imported or exported product, is an _embargo_.

Describe

1.   What is a foreign trade zone?

2.   What are exchange controls and why do governments exercise these controls?

48

3.   What is GATT? What is its general goal?

4.   What are three dimensions of the legal environment for U.S. firms operating abroad?

5.   What is dumping?

Learning Goal 3.8
Explain multinational economic integration. (62-64)

Fill in the Blank

The simplest approach to establishing multinational economic integration is to establish a

free trade area in which participating nations trade freely among themselves without

tariffs or trade restrictions. Each maintains its own tariffs for trade outside this area. A

customs union sets up a free trade area, plus a uniform tariff for trade with

nonmember nations. In a common market economic union, members go beyond a customs union to try to bring about all government trade rules into agreement. These partnerships

meet with varying degrees of success. The ___NAFTA___, which became effective in

1994, created a free-trade zone with the United States, Canada, and Mexico. Perhaps the best-

known example of a common market is that which exists in Europe, called the

european union

Learning Goal 3.9
Distinguish between a global and multinational strategy. (64-65)

---

1. What is the difference between a firm using a global strategy and a firm using a multinational strategy when selling its product?

Name:_____**Professor:**_____

Section:_____**Date:**_____

SELF REVIEW

True or False

___T__ 1.   Since 1987, exports have accounted for more than half of all U.S. economic growth.

___F__ 2.   Exporting is the purchasing of foreign goods, raw materials, and services.

___T__ 3.   Different economic systems have different impacts on the incentives to work and to be productive.

___T__ 4.   In practice, most countries around the world have mixed economies.

___T__ 5.   The balance of trade indicates a nation's exports and imports of goods; the balance of payments indicates the overall flow of money into or out of a country.

___T__ 6.   The devaluation of a country's currency will cause the relative price of its imports to rise and the country will therefore import less.

___F__ 7.   A balance of payments surplus means that more money is leaving the country than entering it.

___T__ 8.   A trade surplus means a country's exports exceed its imports.

___T__ 9.   Specialization and trade based on comparative advantage increases the worldwide supply of all goods traded and therefore countries' standards of living.

___T__ 10.   A joint venture occurs when a firm enters into an agreement with a foreign company or government that specifies the sharing of the operation's costs, risks, management, and profits with the foreign partner.

___F__ 11.   An import quota is a tax levied on products imported from abroad.

___F__ 12.   Dumping is the sale of surplus production in another country at a higher price than that charged in the domestic market.

___F__ 13.   NAFTA is a free trade organization consisting of 12 European countries.

___F__ 14.   A multinational strategy uses a standardized product and marketing strategy worldwide.

52

Multiple Choice

1. Imports:
   a. have accounted for 55 percent of all U.S. economic growth.
   b. on the part of the U.S. represent the production of goods and the supplying of services in a foreign country for sale there or are in other countries.
   c. are purchases of foreign goods, raw materials, and services.
   d. are the sale of domestic goods and services abroad.
   e. are of no concern to U. S. businesses.

2. A mixed economy is best characterized by:
   a. government control over the means of production but free markets determine who gets what is produced.
   b. private ownership over the means of production but the government determines who gets what is produced.
   c. a combination of government ownership and private ownership.
   d. government ownership and operation of key industries but private ownership is allowed for industries that are considered less crucial.
   e. the former Soviet Union.

3. Socialism is:
   a. the same as communism.
   b. characterized by the government owning and operating key industries but private ownership is allowed for industries that are considered less crucial.
   c. more often than not characterized by very low tax rates.
   d. often characterized by very few problems with workers lacking the incentive to work.
   e. all of the above.

4. Privatization:
   a. is the converting of privately held firms into government-owned companies.
   b. has taken place in Mexico and Western Europe by not Eastern Europe.
   c. usually results in a loss of badly needed cash for governments.
   d. is often undertaken to increase the efficiency of industries.
   e. all of the above.

5.   The devaluation of the dollar:
      a.   means the value of the dollar has fallen in international exchange rate markets.
      b.   causes the relative price of U.S. exports to fall and therefore the U.S. exports more.
      c.   causes the relative price of U.S. imports to rise and therefore the U.S. imports less.
      d.   can create a trade surplus.
      e.   all of the above.

6.   A trade deficit:
      a.   means exports exceed imports.
      b.   means imports exceed exports.
      c.   could be caused by a devaluation of a nation's currency.
      d.   will create a larger balance of payments surplus.
      e.   is something the U.S. has never experienced.

7.   If a country has a comparative advantage in the production of good X then:
      a.   it also has an absolute advantage in the production of good X.
      b.   specializing in the production of good X and trading with other nations will reduce the country's standard of living.
      c.   it should import good X.
      d.   it should specialize in the production of good X.
      e.   all of the above.

8.   The most common form of involvement in international business is:
      a.   direct exporting.
      b.   indirect exporting.
      c.   foreign licensing.
      d.   overseas marketing.
      e.   combined foreign production and marketing.

9.   Global business may entail:
      a.   direct exporting which is the least common form of international business.
      b.   foreign licensing which occurs when a firm locates a production facility in a foreign country.
      c.   overseas marketing which is the establishment of a foreign sales office.
      d.   foreign production which is the most common form of international business.
      e.   direct exporting which occurs when a firm allows a foreign company to produce and distribute its products or use its trademarks, patents or processes in a specific geographic area.

10. Countertrade is:
     a. an international bartering agreement in which an exporter must buy something from the country it wishes to sell in.
     b. when a country refuses to allow a foreign product into its borders.
     c. involved in an estimated 90 to 95 percent of all international trade.
     d. a tax on an imported good.
     e. never undertaken by countries with limited foreign exchange or those who are heavily indebted.

11. A tariff is:
     a. a tax levied on products imported from abroad.
     b. a physical limitation on the number of units of a product which can be imported.
     c. a total ban on imported or exported products.
     d. cultural barrier of international trade.
     e. a physical barrier of international trade.

12. The General Agreement on Tariffs and Trade (GATT):
     a. attempts to restrict international trade among countries.
     b. was originally set up to coordinate international financial relations by lending money to countries that require short-term assistance in conducting international trade.
     c. was established to make long-term loans for economic development projects.
     d. helps U.S. firms meet the financing conditions necessary for exporting overseas.
     e. is an international trade accord that has sponsored a series of negotiations that have reduced worldwide tariff levels.

13. The North American Free Trade Agreement (NAFTA):
     a. created a free-trade zone in 1994 between the United States, Mexico and Japan.
     b. created a free-trade zone in 1994 between the United States, Mexico and Europe.
     c. created a free-trade zone in 1994 between the United States, Mexico and Canada.
     d. is not controversial like many other free trade issues.
     e. increases the trade barriers and investment restrictions for its members.

14. If a business undertakes a multinational strategy:
     a. it is choosing to sell a standardized product worldwide.
     b. it is choosing a standardized marketing strategy worldwide.
     c. it is treating each national market differently.
     d. it is not interested in a particular national markets unique tastes or buying habits.
     e. it is lobbying its government to stop the flow of competing imports into the nation.

Name:_____**Professor:**_____

Section:_____**Date:**_____

APPLICATION EXERCISES

1. If a country is going to impose either a tariff or a quota on an imported product, then which do you think would be preferred by the government? Why? Which do you think would be preferred by the foreign business selling the imported product? Why?

2. Assume the exchange rate value of a country's currency rises in international exchange rate markets. What will happen to the relative price of the country's imports and exports? What is expected to happen to the country's amount of imports and exports? Will this create a balance of trade deficit or surplus?

56

3.   To succeed in foreign markets, firms must understand cultural factors, such as language, education, social values, religious attitudes, and consumer habits. Provide some examples of what might constitute international business blunders. If you can't think of any then explain why international businesses must be aware of cultural differences if they wish to be successful in selling their products abroad.

Name:_____ **Professor:**_____
Section:_____ **Date:**_____

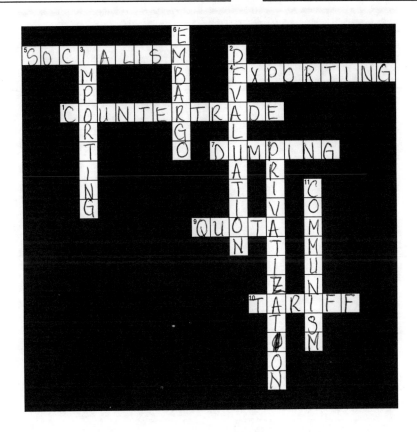

ACROSS

1. An international agreement in which an exporter must buy something in order to buy something else.

4. Selling domestic goods and services abroad.

5. An economic system in which government owns and operates key industries while private ownership is allowed for industries that are considered less crucial.

7. Selling goods abroad at a price lower than that charged in the domestic market. Is prohibited in many countries.

9. A limit on the number of certain products that can be imported.

10. A tax levied on products imported from abroad.

DOWN

2. The fall of a currency's value relative to other currencies or to a fixed standard.

3. Purchasing foreign goods, raw materials, and services.

6. A total ban on imported or exported products.

8. Converting government-owned companies into privately held firms.

11. All property would be shared by the people of a community.

CHAPTER 3 SOLUTIONS

Analysis of Learning Goals

Learning Goal 3.1

1.   At one time the domestic market was all that U.S. firms needed. However, with the growth of technology and more advanced transportation and communication systems there are great opportunities for selling abroad. Opportunities in foreign markets are expanding very rapidly due to their growth and higher standards of living. Moreover, since 1987, exports have accounted for 55 percent of all U.S. growth. Global trade can be expected to be even more important to the U.S. economy in coming years.

2.   a. Exporting   b. Foreign production   c. Importing

Learning Goal 3.2

1. a   2. c   3. d   4. d

Learning Goal 3.3

1. e   5. g
2. d   6. h
3. a   7. f
4. b   8. c

Learning Goal 3.4

1. True   2. True   3. True   4. False

Learning Goal 3.5

1.   Indirect exporting
2.   Direct exporting
3.   Foreign Licensing
4.   Overseas marketing
5.   Combined foreign production and marketing

Learning Goal 3.6

1.   Countertrade is an international bartering agreement in which an exporter must buy something in order to sell something.

2.   A multinational corporation is a firm with major operations outside its home country.

60

Learning Goal 3.7
Cultural barriers
Physical barriers
Tariff
Import quota
Embargo

1.	A foreign trade zone is a special area located at major ports of entry to a country, or important production facilities inland, where foreign goods may be held or processed and then re-exported without incurring further duties (taxes).

2.	Exchange controls are a government's control of its currency. This occurs when firms are allowed to buy and sell currency only through the central bank or other designated government agency. Some governments exercise exchange controls to allocate, expand, or restrict foreign exchange in accordance with national policy. (Sometimes countries do this to restrict the inflow of goods considered as luxuries or unnecessary.)

3.	The General Agreement on Tariffs and Trade (GATT) is an international trade accord that has sponsored a series of negotiations that have reduced worldwide tariff levels. The over-riding goal of GATT is to promote free and open trade because that increases the standard of living for all nations involved in trade.

4.	The legal environment for U.S. firms operating abroad has three dimensions: U.S. law, host-country law, and international requirements. Violations of these legal requirements constitute setbacks for international business and should be carefully avoided.

5.	Dumping is the selling of a good abroad at a price lower than that charged in the domestic market. It is prohibited in many countries because it is considered to be a predatory pricing practice.

Learning Goal 3.8
Free trade area
Customs union
Common market
NAFTA
European Union

Learning Goal 3.9

1.	A global strategy uses a standardized product and marketing strategy worldwide; it sells essentially the same product in the same manner throughout the world. Under a multinational strategy, each national market is treated differently. Firms use a marketing strategy that appeals to the customs, tastes, and buying habits of a particular nation.

Self-Review

True or False

1. T	4. T	7. F	10. T	13. F
2. F	5. T	8. T	11. F	14. F
3. T	6. T	9. T	12. F	

Multiple Choice

1. c	4. d	7. d	10. a	13. c
2. c	5. e	8. b	11. a	14. c
3. b	6. b	9. c	12. e	

Application Exercises

1. The government would probably prefer imposing a tariff because tariffs, being a tax on an imported product, will raise revenues for the government. A quota will not raise any revenues to the government imposing the quota.

    A business would naturally prefer not to have any trade barrier imposed on its product by an importing country. However, if either a tariff or a quota is going to be imposed then it would generally prefer a quota. No tax has to be paid by the business in the event of a quota, compared to a tariff. Moreover, a quota restricts the supply of the product made available in the country. This results in a higher price which can be charged.

2. An increase in a country's exchange rate value for its currency (for example, an increase in the value of the dollar) would create a lower relative price for imports and a higher relative price for exports. (For example, a stronger dollar means a single dollar now buys more units of a foreign currency. Because the imported product is ultimately priced in foreign currency, then the dollar will now buy more units of a foreign product. That is, the imported product's relative price is now lower. Conversely, because it now takes more units of a foreign currency to buy a single dollar then the relative price of American exports is higher.) This, in turn, would cause the country's imports to rise and its exports to fall. The country would then experience movement in the direction of a balance of trade deficit.

3. The following examples are taken from David A. Ricks, Big Business Blunders, Mistakes in Multinational Marketing (Homewood Ill.: Dow Jones Irwin, 1983).
    An airline company placed an advertisement in a Saudi Arabian newspaper displaying what might be considered a "normal" photograph by American standards of an attractive hostess serving champagne to happy airline passengers. However, the photo offended the sensibilities of many people in this Islamic country where alcohol is illegal

and unveiled woman are not permitted to mix with men.

Another example of ignorance of cultural factors occurred in the Middle East where Muslims are forbidden to eat ham. A refrigerator manufacturer displayed a photograph in the print media of a refrigerator with a whole ham placed in a central location inside. The advertisement was viewed as being insensitive and unappealing.

Knowledge of language differences is also important when undertaking international business. General Motors was concerned about the lack of sales of its Chevrolet Nova in Puerto Rico. When literally translated into Spanish, *Nova* means "star." However, when spoken, it sounded like *no va*, Spanish for "it doesn't go." Likewise, Ford introduced a car in Mexico called *Caliente* only to find out later that *caliente* is slang for ""streetwalker" in that country.

Many business blunders could be avoided while other business dealings could be made much more profitable if knowledge of cultural differences are kept firmly in mind.

Crossword Puzzle

CHAPTER 3

Chapter 4

Developing a Business Strategy and Plan

"The time to repair the roof is when the sun is shining." President John F. Kennedy (72)

KEY CONCEPTS

Mission statement	A written explanation of a company's aims. (72)
Objectives	Are guideposts that managers use to define standards of what the organization should accomplish in such areas as profitability, customer service, and employee satisfaction. (73)
Management by objectives (MBO)	MBO encourages employees to participate in setting their own goals, lets them know in advance how they will be evaluated, and bases their performance appraisals on periodic analyses of their progress toward agree-upon goals. (75)
Competitive differentiation	Any aspect of a company or its performance that makes it mort successful than its competitors. (76)
Planning	Planning answers the questions of what should be done, by whom, where, when, and how. (79)
Strategic planning	The process of determining the primary objectives of an organization, adopting courses of action, and allocating the resources necessary to achieve those objectives. (79)
Tactical planning	Involves implementing the activities specified by the strategic plan. (80)
Operational planning	Creates the work standards that implement tactical plans. (80)

64

Adaptive planning	Planning that allows changes in response to new developments in the business's situation and environment. (80)
Contingency planning	Plans to resume operations as quickly and smoothly as possible after a crisis while fully communicating what happened to the public. (80)
Organizing	The means by which management blends human and material resources through a formal structure of tasks and authority. (81)
Directing	Guiding and motivating employees to accomplish organizational objectives. (82)
Controlling	The function of evaluating the organization's performance to determine whether it is accomplishing its objectives. (82)
SWOT analysis	An organized method of assessing a company's internal strengths and weaknesses and external opportunities and threats. (83)
Strategic business units (SBUs)	Each SBU is its own organization, with its own personnel, objectives, and products---and its own planning. (84)
Forecasting	The estimation or prediction of a company's future sales or income. Qualitative forecasting is based on subjective judgement and experience. Quantitative forecasting is based on mathematical models. (84)
Business plan	Description of a business's goals and the means for achieving them. (86)

Name:_____**Professor:**_____
Section:_____**Date:**_____

ANALYSIS OF LEARNING GOALS

Learning Goal 4.1
Differentiation between strategic and tactical planning. (72; 79-80)

---

1.   What is the difference between strategic and tactical planning?

66

Matching

Match the following terms with the statements below.

a. strategic planning
b. tactical planning
c. operational planning
d. adaptive planning

e. contingency planning
f. organizing
g. directing
h. controlling

H 2. The function of evaluating the organization's performance to determine whether it is accomplishing its objectives.

C 3. The creation of work standards that implement tactical plans.

D 4. Planning that allows changes in response to new developments in the business's situation and environment.

A 5. The process of determining the primary objectives of an organization, adopting courses of action, and allocating the resources necessary to achieve those objectives.

G 6. Guiding and motivating employees to accomplish organizational objectives.

E 7. Refers to plans to resume operations as quickly and as smoothly as possible after a crisis while fully communicating what happened to the public.

B 8. Involves implementing the activities specified by the strategic plans.

F 9. Is the means by which management blends human and material resources through a formal structure of tasks and authority.

Learning Goal 4.2
Identify the components of a mission statement. (72-73)

True or False

_____ 1. A mission statement is usually written after the organization has developed its plans and strategies.

__T__ 2. By developing a mission statement, a company can define its general goals and rationale.

__T__ 3. A mission statement may include what products are to be produced and what the market will be, as well as information on treatment of employees and the company's belief system or morals.

__T__ 4. A mission statement is a written explanation of a company's purposes and aims.

Learning Goal 4.3
Define objectives and how they differ from the mission statement. (73-76)

---

1. Define objectives and how they differ from the mission statement.

2. What three important functions do objectives serve for an organization?

    providing direction
    setting standards
    providing motivation.

68

3.   What is a widely used management technique aimed at improving worker motivation and performance which uses objectives at the level of the individual employee? What are some of the benefits and problems with this technique?

Learning Goal 4.4

Define competitive differentiation and identify methods businesses use to create it. (77-79)

Multiple Choice

1.   Competitive differentiation:
    a.   is any aspect of a company or its performance that makes it more successful than its competitors.
    b.   may entail increasing the quality of the company's work force and by creating a more innovative product.
    c.   may entail using efficient up-to-date technology and by reducing overhead and prices.
    d.   all of the above

2.   Which of the following methods of creating competitive differentiation is based on setting quality as a strategic objective and viewing the organization as an entire system with all members contributing to the final results?
    a.   Improving management of human resources.
    b.   Using total quality management.
    c.   Developing new products.
    d.   Using up-to-date technology.

---

3.   Just-in-time logistics:
      a.   can be helpful only for very large firms.
      b.   has not been successful in the United States.
      c.   has been criticized because it can leave a business will no safety cushion in the event of an unforeseen disruption in the flow of needed materials.
      d.   all of the above.

4.   Which of the following statements is true concerning competitive differentiation?
      a.   Few firms benefit from the advances in computer technology because of the cost of that technology.
      b.   It can be accomplished by cutting overhead expenses and prices.
      c.   It can be accomplished by selling a product which is exactly like that of your competitors.
      d.   There are no problems with just-in-time logistics.

Learning Goal 4.5
Explain SWOT analysis and how it is used in corporate planning. (83-84)

---

1.   Explain SWOT analysis and how it is used in corporate planning.

Matching
Match the following terms with the statements below.

a.   leverage
b.   problem
c.   constraint
d.   vulnerable

_A_ 2.   When strengths and opportunities mesh.

_D_ 3.   The combination of an outside threat and an inside strength.

_B_ 4.   When external threats coincide with a company's weaknesses.

_C_ 5.   When opportunity knocks but a firm's weaknesses render it unable to answer.

Learning Goal 4.6
Describe SBUs and give examples. (84)

---

1.   Describe strategic business units (SBUs) and give examples.

Learning Goal 4.7
Define forecasting and differentiate between quantitative and qualitative forecasting. (84)

Fill in the Blank

Forecasting is the estimation or prediction of a company's future sales or income.
They can be short term (under one year), intermediate (one to five years), or long term (over
five years. If the forecasts are subjective and rely on the judgement and opinions of managers,
the sales force, customers, and others then they are Qualitative . On the other
hand, Quantitative forecasts are based on historical data and mathematical
methods.

Learning Goal 4.8
List the methods of forecasting. (84-86)

Listing

List the five types of *qualitative* forecasting techniques.

Sale-Force Composite

1. Sales people are asked to forecast short-term sales based on their extensive knowledge of their territories.

Juryor Executive Opinion

2. An average of the forecasts of top executives from all divisions.

Managerial Opinion

3. During budgeting and planning stages, a manager may be asked to predict the sales results in his or her particular units.

Buyer Surveys

4. Information based on mailed questionnaires and telephone or personal interviews.

Delphi Technicque

5. Uses an anonymous panel of individuals from both outside and inside the company.

List the three types of *quantitative* forecasting techniques.

Trend Anaylsis

6. This method assumes that past performance will repeat itself in the future.

Test Markets

7. Distributes new products in limited areas to assess the best pricing, promotional and packaging strategy.

Exponential Smoothing

8. Analysis of data that considers recent historical data more important than older data.

72

Learning Goal 4.9
Outline the components of the business plan. (86-88)

---

1.   What is a business plan?

2.   Outline the components of the business plan.

Name:_____**Professor:**_____

Section:_____**Date:**_____

SELF REVIEW

True or False

_____1. Tactical planning involves the establishment of actions and the allocation of resources, whereas strategic planning includes implementing the activities specified by the tactical plans.

_____2. Mission statements generally are aimed at guiding the people within a firm, but they also can be used to inform customers of a company's point of view.

_____3. In contrast to the mission statement, which spells out the company's goals in general terms, objectives are more specific and concrete.

_____4. The first step in "management by objectives" is to set short-term performance goals.

_____5. Through the MBO process, the manager and the employee reach an understanding about the employee's major areas of responsibility and required level of performance.

_____6. The chief purpose of management by objectives is to improve employee motivation.

_____7. Just-in-time logistics is a method of streamlining manufacturing or service provision by eliminating wasted time and space.

_____8. Planning is a perpetual process.

_____9. Contingency planning creates the work standards that implement tactical plans.

_____10. Any company can be assessed through SWOT analysis at any point in its history.

_____11. In terms of SWOT analysis a firm is vulnerable when strengths and opportunities mesh.

_____12. Strategic business units (SBUs) are specific objectives within a business plan.

_____13. Qualitative forecasting is based on historical data and mathematical methods.

_____14. A business plan is a written statement of a company's aims.

74

Multiple Choice

1. Tactical planning:
    a. is the means by which management blends human and material resources through a formal structure of tasks and authority.
    —b. involves implementing the activities specified by the strategic plans.
    c. tends to be both broad and long-range, focusing on those organizational objectives that will have a major impact on the organization over several years.
    d. is the actual guiding and motivating of employees to accomplish organizational objectives.
    e. is the function of evaluating the organization's performance to determine whether it is accomplishing its objectives.

2. Controlling refers to:
    a. the function of evaluating the organization's performance to determine whether it is accomplishing its objectives.
    b. the process of determining the primary objectives of an organization, adopting courses of action, and allocating the resources necessary to achieve those objectives.
    c. plans to resume operations as quickly and as smoothly as possible after a crisis while fully communicating what happened to the public.
    d. planning that allows changes in response to new developments in the business's situation and environment.
    e. the means by which management blends human and material resources through a formal structure of tasks and authority.

3. Objectives of a firm:
    a. are more general than a firm's mission statement.
    b. may serve the function of directing the efforts of managers.
    c. are decided upon before writing the mission statement.
    d. are not very helpful in setting tangible benchmarks for evaluating firm performance.
    e. usually reduce the motivation of workers and managers.

4. Management by objectives:
    a. encourages employees to participate in setting their own goals.
    b. lets employees know in advance how they will be evaluated.
    c. bases employees' performance appraisals on periodic analyses of their progress toward agreed-upon goals.
    d. will not succeed unless managers and subordinates feel comfortable with it and are willing to participate in it.
    e. all of the above.

5.	Better customer service, lower employee turnover and pilfering, as well as lower employee recruiting and training costs are likely results of competitive differentiation through improved:
	a.	total quality management.
	b.	management of human resources.
	c.	just-in-time logistics.
	d.	cost reduction.
	e.	product innovation.

6.	Which of the following statements is true about planning?
	a.	Planning answers the questions of what should be done, by whom, where, when, and how.
	b.	Operational planning creates the work standards that implement tactical plans.
	c.	To succeed, companies must include adaptive planning.
	d.	Strategic planning is usually undertaken by top management, tactical planning by middle management, and operational planning by supervisory management.
	e.	All of the above.

7.	Which of the following statements is true?
	a.	The four functions of management are planning, organizing, directing, and controlling.
	b.	Organizing is the means by which management blends human and material resources through a formal structure of tasks and authority.
	c.	Directing is guiding and motivating employees to accomplish organizational objectives.
	d.	Controlling is the function of evaluating the organization's performance to determine whether it is accomplishing its objectives.
	e.	All of the above.

8.	When undertaking SWOT analysis:
	a.	vulnerability is the combination of an outside threat with an inside strength.
	b.	a constraint exists in cases where opportunity knocks but a company's weaknesses render it unable to answer.
	c.	a company has a problem to deal with when external threats mesh with a company's weaknesses.
	d.	leverage exists when strengths and opportunities mesh.
	e.	all of the above.

76

9. Which of the following is a quantitative forecasting technique?
   a. Sales-force composite.
   b. Delphi technique.
   c. Test markets.
   d. Buyer surveys.
   e. Jury of executive opinion.

10. Which of the following forecasting techniques risks tipping off competitors as to a company's plans?
    a. Sales-force composite.
    b. Delphi technique.
    c. Buyer survey.
    d. Test markets.
    e. Trend analysis.

11. A business plan:
    a. is always a formal description of a business's goals and the means for achieving them.
    b. should not include any information about the owner and the managers.
    c. should always be open to revision.
    d. should have a marketing summary which contains an estimate of your monthly cash flow.
    e. should have a financial summary which contains a profile of your average customer.

12. Which of the following is a component of a business plan?
    a. The executive summary.
    b. The marketing plan.
    c. The financial plan.
    d. An evaluation of the business owner, managers, the industry and a discussion of the business's organization and structure.
    e. All of the above.

Name:_____**Professor:**_____
Section:_____**Date:**_____

APPLICATION EXERCISES

1. What are some ways in which a business could differentiate its good and/or service *itself* in order to gain a competitive advantage in the market?

2. Why is it important for people who are thinking about starting a business to draw up a business plan? Who should be involved?

Name:_____ **Professor:**_____

Section:_____ **Date:**_____

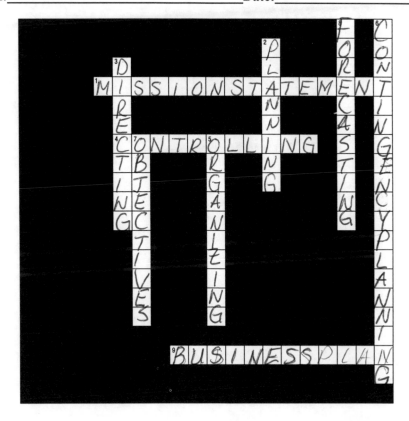

ACROSS

1. A written explanation of a company's aims. (2 words)

4. The function of evaluating the organization's performance to determine whether it is accomplishing its objectives.

9. Description of a business's goals and the means for achieving them. (2 words)

DOWN

2. This answers the questions of what should be done, by whom, where, when, and how.

3. Guiding and motivating employees to accomplish organizational objectives.

5. The means by which management blends human and material resources through a formal structure of tasks and authority.

6. The type of planning designed to resume operations as quickly and smoothly as possible after a crisis while fully communicating what happened to the public. (2 words)

7. Are guideposts that managers use to define standards of what the organization should accomplish in such areas as profitability, customer service, and employee satisfaction.

8. The estimation or predictions of a company's future sales or income. Can be qualitative or quantitative.

CHAPTER 4 SOLUTIONS
Analysis of Learning Goals

Learning Goal 4.1
1. Strategic planning involves the establishment of actions and the allocation of resources, whereas tactical planning includes implementing the activities specified by the strategic plans.
2. h
3. c
4. d
5. a
6. g
7. e
8. b
9. f

Learning Goal 4.2
1. False   2. True   3. True   4. True

Learning Goal 4.3
1. Objectives are guideposts that define standards for what the organization should accomplish in such areas as profitability, customer service, and employee satisfaction. In contrast to the mission statement, which spells out the company's goals in general terms, objectives are more specific and concrete.
2. Objectives serve the function of :
   a) providing direction for managers;
   b) setting standards, or benchmarks for evaluating organizational performance; and
   c) providing motivation by encouraging managers and workers to do their best.

3. A widely used management technique aimed at improving worker motivation and performance which uses objectives at the level of the individual employee is *management by objectives (MBO)*.
   Some of the benefits of using MBO include: a) improving morale by improving communication between employees and managers, b) enabling workers to relate their performance to overall organizational goals, and c) it can serve as a basis for decisions about salary increases and promotions.
   Some of the problems of using MBO include: a) there may be a lack of support and enthusiasm by managers, b) constantly changing goals may make measurement of job performance much more difficult, and c) some managers may have difficulty in communicating with individual employees and in formulating short-term performance goals.

82

Learning Goal 4.4
1. d   2. b   3. c   4. b

Learning Goal 4.5
1.   SWOT analysis is an organized method of assessing a company's internal strengths and weaknesses and external opportunities and threats. SWOT allows the formulation of a practical approach to planning based on a realistic view of a company's situation.
2. a
3. d
4. b
5. c

Learning Goal 4.6
1.   SBUs are divisions within the organization, each with its own executives, workers, objectives, products, and planning. Chevrolet is its Corvette is a SBU of General Motors.

Learning Goal 4.7
Forecasting
Qualitative
Quantitative

Learning Goal 4.8
1. Sales-force composite
2. Jury of executive opinion
3. Managerial opinion
4. Buyer surveys
5. Delphi technique
6. Trend analysis
7. Test markets
8. Exponential smoothing

Learning Goal 4.9
1.   A business plan is a description of a business's goals and the means for achieving them.

2.   The business plan includes the executive summary, the marketing plan, the financial plan, evaluations of the business owner and/or manager and of the industry, and a discussion of the business's organization and structure.

Self-Review

True or False

1. F	4. F	7. T	10. T	13. F
2. T	5. T	8. T	11. F	14. F
3. T	6. T	9. F	12. F	

Multiple Choice

1. b	4. e	7. e	10. d
2. a	5. b	8. e	11. c
3. b	6. e	9. c	12. e

Application Exercises

1. Firms can differentiate their good or service *itself* in either real or imaginary terms. In real terms the business could offer the product at a lower price and/or produce a truly higher quality product. Or, it could change the styling of the product. It could offer a longer guarantee, longer hours of operation, more convenient business locations, free delivery, etc...

    Imaginary differences can also help set a business apart from the pack. However, unlike real differences, there may not be any "scientific" distinction between the company's good and/or service and its competitors. Instead, they are "psychological" differences. The company would be selling an "image."

2. The process of writing a business plan forces one to examine the business thoroughly and objectively in an organized fashion. Written business plans provide an orderly statement for ready reference at all times. They provide guidance, influence, and leadership. They communicate ideas about goals and the means of achieving them to everyone involved.

    Plans usually work best if the whole organization participates because it makes everyone feel a part of the team. When people feel they are part of a team they will work harder to realize the collective goals of the organization.

Crossword Puzzle

CHAPTER 4

Chapter 5

Organizing the Business

"There are three major forms of private business ownership: sole proprietorships, partnerships, and corporations." (94)

KEY CONCEPTS

Sole proprietorship
Ownership (and usually operation) of an organization by one person. (95)

Partnership
An association of two or more persons who operate a business as co-owners by voluntary legal agreement. (95)

Joint venture
A partnership formed for a specific undertaking. (95)

Corporation
A legal organization whose assets and liabilities are separate from those of its owner(s). (96)

Stockholder
Someone who acquires shares of stock in a corporation. (96)

Subsidiary
When all or a majority of a corporation's stock is owned by another corporation. (96)

Board of directors
The governing authority for the corporation. (97)

Merger
Refers to two or more firms that combine to form one company. (97)

Acquisition
When one firm purchases the property and assumes the obligations of another company. (97)

Public ownership
An alternative to private ownership in which a government unit or its agency owns and operates an organization. (98)

Cooperative
An organization whose owners band together to operate all or part of their industries collectively. (98)

Entrepreneur	The risk taker in the private enterprise system, a person who seeks a profitable opportunity and takes the necessary risks to set up and operate a business. (98)
Small business	A firm that is independently owned and operated, is not dominant in its field, and meets certain size standards for its income or number of employees. (99)
Franchising	A business agreement that sets the methods a dealer can use to produce and market a supplier's good or service. (101)
Franchisee	A small-business person who is allowed to sell a good or service of a supplier. Sometimes called a dealer. (101)
Franchisor	Supplier of a franchise that provides various services in exchange for a payment by the franchisee. (101)
Export management company	A domestic firm that specializes in performing international marketing services as commissioned representatives or distributors for other companies. (103)
Export trading company	A general trading firm that plays a varied role in world commerce by importing, exporting, countertrading, investing, and manufacturing. (104)
Small Business Administration (SBA)	The principal government agency concerned with small U.S. firms. (104)

Name:_____ Professor:_____
Section:_____ Date:_____

ANALYSIS OF LEARNING GOALS

Learning Goal 5.1
Identify and explain the three forms of business ownership. (94-97)

Listing

List the form of business ownership referred to by each of the following statements.

Sole Proprietorship 1. The most common form of business ownership.

Partnership 2. When two or more persons who operate a business as co-owners by voluntary legal agreement.

Corporation 3. A legal organization whose assets and liabilities are separate from those of its owner(s).

Partnership 4. The least common form of business ownership.

Corporation 5. This form of business ownership accounts for the largest amount of total output produced by businesses.

Partnership 6. This form of business ownership accounts for approximately 10 percent of U.S. firms.

Sole Proprietor 7. This form of business ownership accounts for approximately 70 percent of U.S. firms.

Corporation 8. This form of business ownership accounts for approximately 20 percent of U.S. firms.

Learning Goal 5.2

Compare the advantages and disadvantages of the forms of business ownership. (94-97)

Fill in the table

List the major advantages and disadvantages associated with each type of business organization.

Form of Ownership	Advantages	Disadvantages
Sole Proprietorship	1. Easy to make 2. Owner keeps all profits 3. Owner has control over aspects	1. Unlimited liability 2. Financing limitations 3. Management 4. Deficincies
Partnership	1. Easy to make 2. Complimentary Management skills 3. Expanded Financial Capacity	1. Unlimited Financial liability 2. Interpersonel conflicts 3. Lack of Continuity

Corporation	1.	1.
	2.	2.
	3.	3.
	4.	

Learning Goal 5.3

Discuss the levels of corporate management. (97-98)

Matching

Match the following levels of management with the statements below.

a. Stockholders
b. Board of directors
c. Top management
d. Middle management
e. Supervisory management

A 1. They buy shares of stock in the corporation and elect the board of directors.

C 2. They manage overall operations, make major decisions, and introduce major changes.

E 3. They coordinate day-to-day operations, supervise employees, and evaluate staff performance.

D 4. They manage operations and serve as liaison between top management and other levels.

B 5. They set overall policy, authorize major transactions, and hire the CEO.

Learning Goal 5.4

Explain how private ownership, public ownership,
and collective ownership (cooperatives) differ. (98)

Fill in the Blank

Private Ownership refers to ownership by an individual or individuals, regardless

of whether the organization is set up as a sole proprietorship, partnership, or corporation. One

alternative to this form of ownership is *Public Ownership*, in which a

government unit or its agency owns and operates an organization on behalf of the population

served by the unit. Another form of ownership is the *Cooperative* , which

provides for collective ownership of production, storage, transportation, and/or marketing

activities.

Learning Goal 5.5

Explain the vital role played by entrepreneurs and small businesses in the global economy.
(98-99)

---

1. Why is entrepreneurship and the presence of small businesses important in a free
    enterprise system?

Learning Goal 5.6
Define small business and identify the industries in which most small firms are established.
(99)

---

1.   Define small business and identify the industries in which most small firms are established.

Learning Goal 5.7
Compare the advantages and disadvantages of small business. (99-100)

---

1.   What are the advantages of small businesses?

2.   What are the disadvantages of small businesses?

92

Learning Goal 5.8
Describe resources that are available to entrepreneurs. (104)

---

1.   Describe resources that are available to entrepreneurs if they want help in starting a business.

Learning Goal 5.9
List the advantages and disadvantages of franchising. (101-102)

Multiple Choice

1.   One of the advantages of buying into a franchise is:
      a.   that good ones usually sell for more.
      b.   the corporate culture which has already been established.
      c.   that when some franchises outlets fail, this can effect consumers' attitude toward all the outlets.
      d.   the widely recognized name the franchise offers.

2.   One of the disadvantages of franchising is:
      a.   the performance record on which the prospective buyer can make comparisons and judgements.
      b.   a tested management system.
      c.   the restrictions that come from fitting into an established corporate culture.
      d.   a widely recognized name.

Learning Goal 5.10
Outline the popular methods of small business operation in the global market. (103-104)

True or False

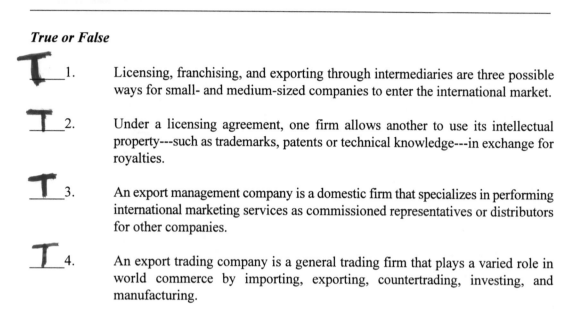

T 1.   Licensing, franchising, and exporting through intermediaries are three possible ways for small- and medium-sized companies to enter the international market.

T 2.   Under a licensing agreement, one firm allows another to use its intellectual property---such as trademarks, patents or technical knowledge---in exchange for royalties.

T 3.   An export management company is a domestic firm that specializes in performing international marketing services as commissioned representatives or distributors for other companies.

T 4.   An export trading company is a general trading firm that plays a varied role in world commerce by importing, exporting, countertrading, investing, and manufacturing.

Name:_____Professor:_____
Section:_____Date:_____

SELF REVIEW
True or False

T   1.   Corporations are generally considered to have the greatest advantages relative to its disadvantages.

F   2.   The greatest number of real world businesses are corporations.

F   3.   A major disadvantage of corporations is the unlimited liability of owners.

T   4.   A joint venture is a partnership formed for a specific undertaking.

F   5.   A merger occurs when one firm purchases the property and assumes the obligations of another; an acquisition is when two or more firms combine to form one company.

F   6.   A cooperative is a form of ownership in which a government unit or its agency owns and operates an organization on behalf of the population served by the unit.

T   7.   The entrepreneur is the risk taker in the private enterprise system, a person who seeks a profitable opportunity and takes the necessary risks to set up and operate a business.

F   8.   Almost every single small businesses is found in the services industry.

T   9.   On average, nearly 62% of all businesses dissolve within the first six years.

T   10.   Most small businesses are started by women and minorities.

T   11.   The most common types of businesses owned by women and minorities are service and retail firms.

F   12.   The greatest financial obstacle facing small businesses is taxes.

F   13.   The Small Business Administration (SBA) is a federal government agency charged with the responsibility of collecting taxes from small businesses.

T   14.   When a franchise is purchased the buyer is called the franchisee, the seller is called the franchisor.

96

Multiple Choice

1.   The fewest number of real-world businesses are:
     a.   sole proprietorships.
     b.   partnerships.
     c.   corporations.
     d.   small businesses.
     e.   small business administrations.

2.   Which of the following is a major disadvantage associated with sole proprietorships?
     a.   Unlimited financial liability.
     b.   Tax disadvantage.
     c.   Legal restrictions.
     d.   Difficult and costly to form and dissolve.
     e.   Interpersonal conflicts among owners of the business.

3.   Which of the following is an advantage associated with corporations?
     a.   Easy to form and dissolve.
     b.   Owner retains all profits after taxes.
     c.   Limited financial liability.
     d.   Owner has control over all aspects of the business.
     e.   Tax advantage.

4.   Partnerships are characterized by:
     a.   being difficult and costly to form.
     b.   the absence of potential interpersonal conflicts.
     c.   limited financial liability of owners.
     d.   unlimited financial liability by each partner for the debts of the firm.
     e.   being extremely easy to dissolve.

5.   The board of directors in corporate management:
     a.   are the shareholders (stockholders) in the corporation.
     b.   manage overall operations, make major decisions, and introduce major changes.
     c.   coordinate day-to-day operations, supervise employees, and evaluate staff performance.
     d.   manage operations and serve as liaison between top management and other levels.
     e.   set overall policy, authorize major transactions, and hire the CEO.

6.   The entrepreneur is a:
    a.   supervisory manager in a corporation.
    b.   stockholder in a corporation.
    c.   CEO in a corporation
    d.   risk taker in the private enterprise system, a person who seeks a profitable opportunity and takes the necessary risks to set up and operate a business.
    e.   all of the above.

7.   A small business is:
    a.   one that is owned and operated independently.
    b.   does not dominate its market.
    c.   is relatively small for its income and number of employees.
    d.   is found in nearly every industry, including farming, retailing, services, and high technology.
    e.   all of the above.

8.   An advantage of buying into a franchise is:
    a.   the performance record on which the prospective buyer can make comparisons and judgements.
    b.   a tested management system.
    c.   the widely recognized name the franchise offers.
    d.   all of the above.
    e.   none of the above.

9.   Licensing is when a firm:
    a.   plays a varied role in world commerce by importing, exporting, countertrading, investing, and manufacturing.
    b.   specializes in performing international marketing services as commissioned representatives or distributors for other companies.
    c.   allows another firm to use its intellectual property---such as a trademark, patent, or technical knowledge---in exchange for royalties.
    d.   sells its franchise to another firm.
    e.   registers itself as a corporation with the Department of State.

10.   One of the small- and medium-sized companies can enter into the international market is by:
    a.   licensing.
    b.   franchising.
    c.   exporting.
    d.   all of the above
    e.   none of the above.

Name:_____**Professor:**_____

Section:_____**Date:**_____

APPLICATION EXERCISES

1.   As an up and coming business expert you consult people, for a small fee, whom are interested in starting their own businesses. You provide advise with respect to the legal form which their businesses ought to take, given their individual circumstances. Which form of business would you recommend to the following clients? Why?

   a.   Elynn Ridens has been a very dependable manager of a large grocery store's floral shop for years. She has enjoyed working directly with the public and gets along with   everyone. She is good at designing floral arrangements but doesn't particularly like doing paper work. Although she enjoys her current position and its security her desire for a bigger challenge and an opportunity to more fully express her independence has had her thinking about opening her own floral shop for years. She is very confident that her own floral shop would be very prosperous. However, she lacks some of the financial resources to get started.

   b.   Susan Broderick is a talented computer scientist and software designer whom has developed a name for herself in Silicon Valley. She has recently become troubled with the apparent lack of willingness on the part of her current employer to take the long term monetary risks necessary to invest in her latest software development ideas. She claims that the short-sightedness on the part of her employer may result in the company losing out on a vast new market for software technology and huge potential profits. She is willing to put up a lot of money to invest in the creation of a new company but she is not willing to lose all that she has gained over the years. What she can invest in the creation of a new business is still far from the funds necessary to undertake the research and development which will be required to develop this next generation of software capabilities. Moreover, she only wants to undertake the research and development---not the day-to-day management of the firm.

100

c. Scott Kohrs is a highly motivated young man who wants to be his own boss. He has been making his current boss a lot of money as a house painter for quite some time. Because of his reputation in the community of being an excellent and dependable painter he is convinced he could make even more money for himself if he could run his own house-painting business. He already has the equipment and the funds necessary to get started. His insurance and operating expenses are expected to be relatively very small.

2. How is a corporate income taxed twice?

Name:_____Professor:_____
Section:_____Date:_____

CROSSWORD PUZZLE

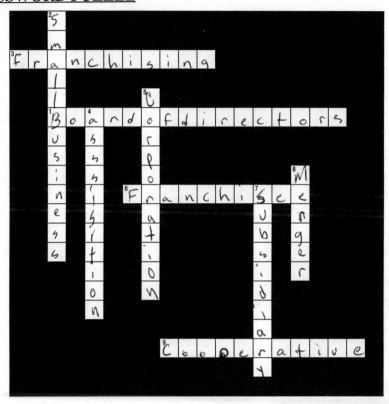

ACROSS

1. The governing body for the corporation. (3 words)

3. A business agreement that sets the methods a dealer can use to produce and market a supplier's good or service.

6. A small-business person who is allowed to sell a good or service of a supplier. Sometimes called a dealer.

9. An organization whose owners band together to operate all or part of their industries collectively.

DOWN

2. A firm that is independently owned and operated, is not dominant in its field, and meets certain size standards for its income or number of employees. (2 words)

4. When one firm purchases the property and assumes the obligations of another company.

5. A legal organization whose assets and liabilities are separate from those of its owner(s) and innovations.

7. When all or a majority of a corporation's stock is owned by another corporation.

8. Refers to two or more firms that combine to form one company.

CHAPTER 5 SOLUTIONS

Analysis of Learning Goals

Learning Goal 5.1
1. Sole proprietorship
2. Partnership
3. Corporation
4. Partnership
5. Corporation
6. Partnership
7. Sole proprietorship
8. Corporation

Learning Goal 5.2

Form of Ownership	Advantages	Disadvantages
Sole Proprietorship	1. Easy to form and dissolve 2. Owner has control over all aspects 3. Owner retains all profits after taxes	1. Unlimited liability 2. Financing limitations 3. Management deficiencies 4. Lack of continuity
Partnership	1. Easy to form 2. Complementary management skills 3. Expanded financial capacity	1. Unlimited financial liability 2. Interpersonal conflicts 3. Lack of continuity
Corporation	1. Limited financial liability 2. Specialized management skills 3. Expanded financial capacity 4. Economies of larger scale operation	1. Difficult and costly to form and dissolve 2. Tax disadvantage 3. Legal restrictions.

Learning Goal 5.3
1. a   2. c   3. e   4. d   5. b

104

Learning Goal 5.4
Private ownership
Public ownership
Cooperative (Collective ownership)

Learning Goal 5.5
1.   Entrepreneurs and a strong small business sector provide the competitive zeal that keeps a private enterprise system vibrant. Small businesses also help other businesses function more efficiently because they often tend to specialize and offer greater expertise in a particular area.

Learning Goal 5.6
1.   A small business is one that is owned and operated independently, does not dominate its market, and meets a variety of size standards for its income or number of employees. Small companies are found in nearly every industry, including farming, retailing, services, and high technology.

Learning Goal 5.7
1.   Advantages of small businesses include the ease of introduction of innovations, the ability to provide better service and lower costs, and the ability to fill isolated niche markets.

2.   The disadvantages include inadequate or poor management skills, inadequate financing, and government regulation.

Learning Goal 5.8
1.   The Small Business Administration (SBA) is the principal government agency concerned with promoting the creation of small U.S. firms. The SBA provides financial assistance, aids in government procurement matters, and offers management training and consulting. Other resources for financing include Small Business Investment Companies and venture capitalists.

Learning Goal 5.9
1. d   2. c

Learning Goal 5.10
1. True   2. True   3. True   4. True

Self-Review

True or False

1. T	4. T	7. T	10. T	13. F
2. F	5. F	8. F	11. T	14. T
3. F	6. F	9. T	12. F	

Multiple Choice

1. b	4. d	7. e	10. d
2. a	5. e	8. d	
3. c	6. d	9. c	

Application Exercises

1.   a.   Partnership. A very reliable and very dependable partner (remember there is unlimited liability) which likes to do paperwork and who has the needed funds to get started would be ideal.

       b.   Corporation. There is a need for large sums of money , she wants limited liability and doesn't want to run the company on a day-to-day basis although she would want enough control over the stock to influence investment decisions. Moreover, her reputation should help the chances of selling stock in the first place and for the corporation to raise funds later.

       c.   Sole proprietorship. Because he wants to be his own boss, there is little need for outside sources of funds and virtually no chance of losing personal property in the event of business failure.

2.   Corporate income is taxed twice. First, corporate income taxes have to be paid by the corporation itself. Second, if the corporation pays dividends to stockholders (owners of the corporation) then that income is taxed again as personal income.

Crossword Puzzle

CHAPTER 5

Chapter 6
The Role of Quality in Business Success

"Managing for quality to provide complete customer satisfaction is essential for surviving and thriving in today's competitive global marketplace." (110)

KEY CONCEPTS

Quality	The degree of excellence or superiority of an organization's goods and services. (110)
Customer satisfaction	The concept that a good or service pleases buyers because it meets their emotional needs and quality expectations. (111)
Total quality management (TQM)	An approach that involves a commitment to quality in achieving world-class performance and customer satisfaction as a crucial strategic objective. (111)
ISO 9000	International standards for quality management and quality assurance. (113)
Statistical quality control	A system using statistical procedures to gather and analyze data to pinpoint and correct problem areas. (115)
External customers	People or organizations who buy or use another firm's good or service. (116)
Internal customers	Individual employees or entire departments within an organization who depend on the work of other people or departments to perform their jobs. (116)
Feedback	Messages returned by the audience to the sender that may cause the sender to alter or cancel an original message. (120)
Continuous process improvement	The process of constantly studying and making changes in work activities to improve their quality, timeliness, efficiency, and effectiveness. (121)

108

Cycle time

The time it takes to complete a work process or activity from beginning to end. (121

Reengineering

The process of mapping out delivery chain processes in detail to identify areas in which to reduce cycle time or errors by applying technology in those key steps. (122)

PDCA cycle

A step-by-step process of **P**lanning, **D**oing, **C**hecking, and **A**cting. (122)

Costs of quality

Costs associated with poor-quality products and production processes, such as scrap, rework, and loss of customers. (123)

Benchmarking

Identifying how business leaders achieve superior performance levels in their industry and continuously compare and measure the firm's performance against these outstanding performers. (123)

Critical success factors

Activities and functions considered most important in gaining a competitive advantage and achieving long-term success. (125)

Employee involvement

Practices that motivate employees to perform their jobs better through empowerment, training, and teamwork. (127)

Empowerment

The practice of giving employees the authority to make decisions about their work without supervisory approval. (127)

Quality circle

A small group of employees from one work area or department who meet regularly to identify and solve problems. (128)

Cross-functional team

Involves employees from different departments who work on specific projects, such as developing a new product or solving a complex problem. (128)

Self-managed team

A group of employees who work with little or no supervision. (128)

Name:_____**Professor:**_____

Section:_____**Date:**_____

ANALYSIS OF LEARNING GOALS

Learning Goal 6.1

Explain the importance of quality and customer satisfaction in achieving a competitive advantage. (110-112)

---

1.   What is quality?

2.   What is meant by customer satisfaction?

3.   Why is quality and customer satisfaction important in achieving a competitive advantage?

4.   What is total quality management (TQM)?

110

Learning Goal 6.2
Summarize the status of quality programs in the United States, Japan, and Europe. (112-113)

True or False

F 1. Although the Malcolm Baldridge National Quality Award was introduced in the United States in 1987 to promote quality improvement in America, there has been no sign of increasing quality in American made goods and services.

T 2. Japan has become a world leader in quality by studying the work of American quality consultants such as W. Edwards Deming.

F 3. The quality of goods and services produced in Europe are not much of a match to those produced in the United States or Japan.

F 4. ISO 9000 is an organization of the leading 9000 firms in the world with proven quality track records.

Learning Goal 6.3
Discuss the role of top management in applying total quality management (TQM) to an organization. (114-115)

True or False

T 1. Effective TQM begins with the involvement of top managers who believe in the importance of quality and customer satisfaction.

F 2. Managers should view their departments within their organizations as individual entities so they can be analyzed independently from the larger organization.

T 3. Managers are responsible for communicating the goals of total quality management to all staff members.

T 4. Managers should encourage employees to improve themselves and to take pride in their work.

Learning Goal 6.4

Relate TQM to various functions within an organization, including production, human resource management, marketing, information processes, and financial management.
(115-120)

Matching

Match the following functions within an organization to the TQM approach within that function as indicated by the following statements.

a.   The production process
b.   Human resource management
c.   The market function

d.   Information processes
e.   Financial management

A 1.   Improving quality through statistical quality control.

E 2.   Setting clear quality goals and linking them to monetary returns and employee compensation.

C 3.   Improving product design, distribution strategy, promotion, and price competitiveness.

B 4.   Motivating workers and offering helpful services to employees.

D 5.   Improving customer services and boosting employees' productivity.

Learning Goal 6.5

Identify the major methods of securing feedback from customers, employees, and suppliers.
(120-121)

1.   What is feedback and why is it important in improving quality?

112

Listing

Supplier feedback 2. A method of securing feedback which thinks in terms of customer/supplier partnerships.

Employee 3. Effective managers take time to solicit and respond feedback, either formally or informally, from within the organization.

Customer 4. The type of feedback where gaps between actual quality and perceived quality may exist.

Learning Goal 6.6

Describe how organizations can work toward continuous process improvement. (121-124)

Multiple Choice

1. Continuous process improvement:
   a. is called *kaizen* in Japanese.
   b. is the process of constantly studying and making changes in work activities to improve their quality, timeliness, efficiency, and effectiveness.
   c. must be ongoing.
   d. all of the above.

2. Continuous process improvement focuses on:
   a. reducing cycle time.
   b. reducing variation.
   c. eliminating waste.
   d. all of the above.

3. Cycle time is:
   a. is the time it takes to complete a work process or activity, from beginning to end.
   b. increases the time it takes to bring new products to the market.
   c. reduces the firm's ability to respond quickly in filling customers' orders.
   d. all of the above.

4.   Reducing variation in the production and delivery of a good or service is:
        a.   much more difficult for equipment-based providers than people-based providers.
        b.   not likely to be improved with statistical controls.
        c.   much more cost effective than inspecting finished products to spot defects and then correcting problems.
        d.   all of the above.

5.   Eliminating waste :
        a.   means eliminating any work activity that does not add value to the product.
        b.   internally is easier to measure than eliminating waste externally.
        c.   is usually not worthwhile because it usually does not save a company much money.
        d.   all of the above.

Learning Goal 6.7
Define benchmarking and explain its contributions to quality and customer satisfaction.
(124-126)

---

1.   Define benchmarking and explain its contributions to quality and customer satisfaction.

114

Matching
Match the five steps in the benchmarking process with the descriptive statements which follow.

a.   Planning phase   d.   Action phase
b.   Analysis phase   e.   Maturity phase
c.   Integration phase

A 2.   Selecting benchmarking candidates; identifying organizations to use in making comparisons; and selecting data-collection methods and collecting needed data.

C 3.   Communicating benchmarking findings and gaining acceptance; establishing functional goals; and developing action plans.

B 4.   Identifying gaps between company practices and industry-best practices; and forecasting future performance levels if identified benchmarks are implemented.

E 5.   Achievement of leadership position; benchmarking is fully integrated throughout the organization.

D 6.   Implementing plans and monitoring progress; reviewing benchmarks and replace them as needed.

Learning Goal 6.8
Identify the components of employee involvement and their impact on quality and customer satisfaction. (127-128)

Fill in the Blank

Employee involvement refers to practices that motivate employees to perform their jobs better through empowerment, training and teamwork. *Empowerment* is the practice of giving employees the authority to make decisions about their work without supervisory approval. Employee *Training* consists of a wide variety of learning experiences. The value of *teamwork* is that, by working collectively, employees produce higher performance levels, respond more quickly, and become more flexible to customer needs.

Name:_____   Professor:_____

Section:_____   Date:_____

SELF REVIEW

True or False

___T___ 1.   Quality-conscious companies involve employees in every business function in understanding and satisfying customer needs and wants.

___F___ 2.   Total quality management (TQM) is a concept that a good or service pleases buyers because it meets their emotional needs and quality expectations.

___T___ 3.   ISO 9000 are international standards established in the European Union for quality management and quality assurance.

___F___ 4.   Firms producing higher quality products are able to increase their sales but almost always experience higher costs and as a consequence must charge higher prices.

___T___ 5.   Statistical quality control is a system using statistical procedures to gather and analyze data to pinpoint and correct problem areas.

___F___ 6.   Internal customers are people or organizations who buy or use another firm's good or service.

___T___ 7.   As a first step in improving quality, a company must compile feedback to use in measuring its present performance.

___T___ 8.   Reengineering and the PDCA cycle are tools for identifying ways to reduce cycle time and errors.

___T___ 9.   Costs of quality are the costs associated with poor-quality products and production processes, such as scrap, rework, and loss of customers.

___F___ 10.   Benchmarking is the practice of giving employees the authority to make decisions about their work without supervisory approval.

___T___ 11.   Critical success factors are the activities and functions considered most important in gaining a competitive advantage and achieving long-term success.

___F___ 12.   Empowerment of employees occurs when workers own the company.

___F___ 13.   A quality circle is a group of employees who work with little or no supervision.

116

Multiple Choice

1. Which of the following statements is true?
    a. Companies committed to quality are so customer-focused that they manage their businesses according to their customers' definition of quality.
    b. Quality describes the degree of excellence or superiority of an organization's goods and services.
    c. Customer satisfaction is the concept that a good or service pleases buyers because it meets their emotional needs and quality expectations.
    d. Total quality management (TQM) is an approach that involves a commitment to quality in achieving world-class performance and customer satisfaction as a crucial strategic objective.
    e. All of the above.

2. ISO 9000 is:
    a. the most coveted award one can receive for producing a high quality product in Europe.
    b. the most coveted award one can receive for producing a high quality product in Japan.
    c. the most coveted award one can receive for producing a high quality product in the United States
    d. is a widely recognized quality model established in Europe.
    e. not important for U.S. exporters to be aware of.

3. Total Quality management (TQM):
    a. is primarily concerned with increasing efficiency on the shop floor.
    b. is effective only if it starts with a firm commitment and an involvement of top management.
    c. argues against managers viewing their organizations as systems.
    d. means managers do not have to communicate the goal of quality to employees.
    e. means managers do not have to encourage workers to improve themselves or to take pride in their work.

4. Internal quality improvements will likely:
    a. decrease productivity.
    b. increase costs.
    c. result in a higher priced good or service.
    d. increase market share.
    e. do all of the above.

5.   Which function within an organization is a firm trying to support TQM programs if it is using an effective motivational technique centered on the concepts of internal and external customers?

     a.   The production process.

     b.   Human resource management.

     c.   The marketing function.

     d.   The information process.

     e.   Financial management.

6.   In which type of feedback do company's often use surveys and toll-free telephone lines?

     a.   Manager feedback.

     b.   Supplier feed back.

     c.   Customer feed back.

     d.   Employee feedback.

     e.   Government feedback.

7.   Which of the following statements is true with respect to continuous process improvement?

     a.   To be effective it must be an ongoing process.

     b.   It focuses on reducing cycle time, reducing variation, and eliminating waste.

     c.   It is the process of constantly studying and making changes in work activities to improve their quality, timeliness, efficiency, and effectiveness.

     d.   It involves more than making the production line more efficient.

     e.   All of the above.

8.   Costs of quality are defined as:

     a.   the higher costs of production to ensure a higher quality product.

     b.   the costs of Planning, Doing, Checking, and Acting.

     c.   the costs associated with poor-quality products and production processes, such as scrap, rework, and loss of customers.

     d.   the higher costs imposed on customers in the form of a higher priced product.

     e.   all of the above.

118

9. Which of the following statements is true?
    a. Cycle time is the time it takes to complete a work process or activity, from beginning to end.
    b. Reducing variation in the production and delivery of a good or service is much more difficult for people-based providers than equipment-based providers of goods and services.
    c. Reducing variation is much more cost effective than inspecting finished products to spot defects and then correcting problems.
    d. Eliminating waste means eliminating any work activity that does not add value to the product.
    e. All of the above.

10. Which of the following statements is true regarding benchmarking?
    a. The benchmarking product should focus on critical success factors.
    b. Benchmarking is a customer feedback tool.
    c. Benchmarking is a coveted award presented in Europe in recognition of the production of a high quality product.
    d. Benchmarking findings are not very helpful in implementing improvements.
    e. The maturity phase of the benchmarking process consists of the selecting of benchmarking candidates.

11. Which of the following is *not* a step in the benchmarking process?
    a. The dominant phase.
    b. The analysis phase.
    c. The integration phase.
    d. The planning phase.
    e. The action phase.

12. The practice of giving employees the authority to make decisions about their work without supervisory approval is called:
    a. a quality circle.
    b. employee training.
    c. empowerment.
    d. teamwork.
    e. benchmarking.

Name:_____**Professor:**_____
Section:_____**Date:**_____

APPLICATION EXERCISES

1.   Which of Deming's "14 Points for Quality" are most important? Which of these 14 points do you think most U.S. business firms are lacking?

2.   Are the successful business practices and techniques used to enhance quality production in other countries, like Japan, transplantable to U.S. firms? Why or why not?

Name:_____Professor:_____

Section:_____Date:_____

CROSSWORD PUZZLE

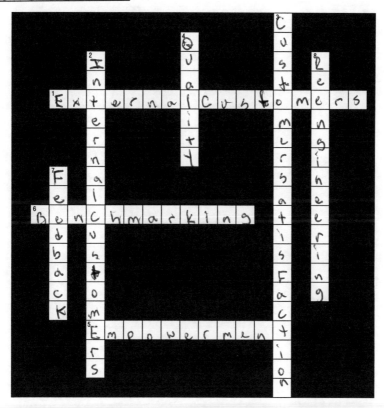

ACROSS

1. People or organiztions who buy or use another firm's good or service.

5. The practice of giving employees the authority to make decision about their work without supervisory approval.

6. Identifying how business leaders achieve superior performance levels in their industry and continuously compare and measure the firm's performance against these outstanding performers.

DOWN

2. Individual employees or entire departments within an organization who depend on the work of other people or departments to perform their jobs.

3. The concept that a good or service pleases buyers because it meets their emotional needs and quality expectations.

4. The degree of excellence or superiority of an organization's goods or services.

7. Messages returned by the audience to the sender that may cause the sender to alter or cancel an original message.

8. The process of mapping out delivery chain processes in detail to identify areas in which to reduce cycle time or errors by applying technology in those key steps.

CHAPTER 6 SOLUTIONS

Analysis of Learning Goals

Learning Goal 6.1

1. Quality describes the degree of excellence or superiority of an organization's goods and services.

2. Customer satisfaction is the concept of a good or service pleasing buyers because if has met their emotional needs and quality expectations. The true measure of quality is whether a business has satisfied its customers.

3. Quality and customer satisfaction directly effect the bottom line and are crucial to an organization's continued existence, both domestically and internationally.

4. Total quality management (TQM) is an approach that involves a commitment to quality in achieving world-class performance and customer satisfaction as a crucial strategic objective.

Learning Goal 6.2

1. False   2. True   3. False   4. False

Learning Goal 6.3

1. True   2. False   3. True   4. True

Learning Goal 6.4

1. a   2. e   3. c   4. b   5. d

Learning Goal 6.5

1. Feedback are messages returned by the audience to the sender that may cause the sender to alter or cancel an original message. Feedback is a first step in improving quality. A company must compile feedback to use in measuring its present performance.

2. Supplier feedback
3. Employee feedback
4. Customer feedback

Learning Goal 6.6

1. d   2. d   3. a   4. c   5. a

124

Learning Goal 6.7

1.   Benchmarking is the process in which an organization continuously compares and measures itself against business leaders anywhere in the world, to gain information that will help it improve its performance. It can be applied to all business procedures and practices.

2. a   3. c   4. b   5. e   6. d

Learning Goal 6.8

Empowerment
Training
Teamwork

Self-Review

True or False

1. T	4. F	7. T	10. F	13. F
2. F	5. T	8. T	11. T	
3. T	6. F	9. T	12. F	

Multiple Choice

1. e	4. d	7. e	10. a
2. d	5. b	8. c	11. a
3. b	6. c	9. e	12. c

Application Exercises

1.   According to Deming all of the 14 points are equally important to a systemic change which is required if a firm is to truly undertake TQM as its approach to doing business. One cannot stand without the others.

       As to which of these 14 points may be most lacking in most U.S. businesses is difficult to say. It depends upon the industry, as well as the particular firm investigated within any given industry. This question was designed to generate thought. There is no "correct" answer.

2.   Some successful business practices and techniques used to enhance quality production in other countries are transplantable to U.S. firms. Some may have more difficulty being used in the United States. This is because of the different social, cultural, historical and governmental factors one finds in the United States. Nevertheless, one should always be on the lookout for a better way.

Crossword Puzzle

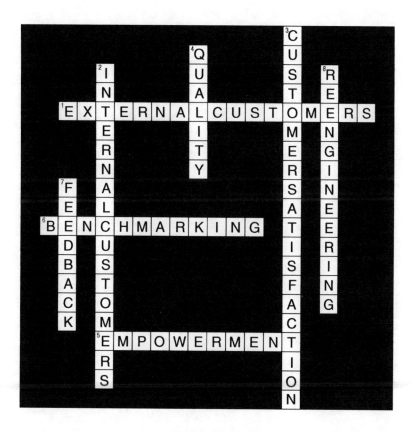

CHAPTER 6

The Organization and Its Management

"The importance of effective management
to organizational success cannot be overestimated." (136)

KEY CONCEPTS

Management	The achievement of organizational objectives through people and other resources. (136)
Top management	The highest level of the management hierarchy and is staffed by executives who develop long-range plans and interact with the public and outside entities, like the government. (137)
Middle management	Managers responsible for developing detailed plans and procedures to implement the general plans of top management. (137)
Supervisory management	People who are directly responsible for the details of assigning workers to specific jobs and evaluating performance. Often referred to as first-line managers. (137)
Organization	A structured grouping of people working together to achieve organizational objectives. (138)
Delegation	The act of assigning activities to subordinates. (140)
Downsizing	Management decides to eliminate layers from the management hierarchy in an effort to reduce costs and make the firm more efficient. (142)
Empowering	Giving employees additional decision-making authority and responsibility. (143)
Outsourcing	Relying on outside specialists to perform functions previously performed by company employees. (144)

128

Line organization	Organization based on the direct flow of authority from the chief executive to subordinates. (144)
Line-and-staff organization	Combines the direct flow of authority present in the line organization with staff departments that serve, advise, and support the line departments. (145)
Matrix, or Project management organization	A structure in which specialists from different parts of the organization are brought together to work on specific projects. (146)
Technical skills	The manager's ability to understand and use techniques, knowledge, and tools of a specific discipline or department. (148)
Human relation skills	Ability to work effectively with and through people. (148)
Conceptual skills	Ability to see the organization as a unified whole and understand how each part of the overall organization interacts with other parts. (149)
Leadership	Act of motivating or causing others to perform activities designed to achieve specific objectives. (150)
Corporate culture	The value system of an organization. (151)
Intrapreneurship	Entrepreneurial-type activity within the corporate culture. (152)
Decision-making	Involves recognizing that a problem exists, identifying it, evaluating alternatives, selecting and implementing an alternative, and following up. (152)
Time management	The effective allocation of one's time among different tasks. (153)

Name:_____**Professor:**_____
Section:_____**Date:**_____

ANALYSIS OF LEARNING GOALS

Learning Goal 7.1
*Discuss the need for an organizational structure,
and list the stops involved in the organizing process.* (138-142)

Fill in the Blank

The achievement of organizational objectives through people and other resources is known as

Management_____. A firm's management can be divided into three levels. The highest level

of management, concerned with developing long-range plans, and interacting with the public and

outside entities is known as Top Management. The level of management concerned with

developing detailed plans and procedure to implement the general plans of top management is

known as Middle Management People who are concerned with the details of assigning

workers to specific jobs and evaluating performance daily or even hourly is the concern of

Supervisory Management_____. Effective human relation skills are particularly important for

Supervisory Management.

Listing

The following statements describe the 5 steps involved in the organizing process. Determine
whether each of the following statements refers to the first, second, third, fourth or fifth step.

130

First 1. Determine specific work activities necessary to implement plans and achieve objectives.

Third 2. Assign activities to specific positions and people and allocate necessary resources.

Fifth 3. Evaluate results of the organizing process.

Second 4. Group work activities into a logical pattern or structure.

Fourth 5. Coordinate activities of different groups and individuals.

Learning Goal 7.2
Evaluate each of the four basic forms of organization. (144-147)

Matching

Match the four following forms of organization to each of the statements below.

a. Line organization
b. Line-and-staff organization

c. Committee organization
d. Matrix (Project management) organization

_A_ 1. This is the simplest form of organization, but it suffers form a lack of specialization of management.

_A_ 2. This form of organization is based on a direct flow of authority from the chief executives to subordinates.

_C_ 3. This form of organization rarely is used as the sole organization structure, but it is incorporated to some extent within the line-and-staff structure.

_D_ 4. This form of organizational structure permits large, multiproduct firms to focus organizational resources on specific problems or projects.

_B_ 5. This form of organization assigns authority to managers and adds specialists to provide information and advice to the managers.

_D_ 6. Because of its "team" approach and the fact that team members are accountable to more than one manager, conflict can occur.

<u>C</u> 7.   This form of organization is noted for being particularly slow in making decisions, which often end up being compromises among conflicting interests.

<u>B</u> 8.   Conflict can arise in this form of organization between managers and specialists if their relationship is unclear.

Learning Goal 7.3
Identify the skills required for managerial success. (147-150)

Listing

List the three basic managerial skills required for managerial success.

<u>Technical Skills</u>   1.   These skills involve the manager's ability to understand and use techniques, tools, and knowledge of a specific discipline or department, and are most important for first-level managers.

<u>Human Relation Skills</u>   2.   These skills involve working effectively with and through people in the accomplishment of assignments, and are important for managers at every level.

<u>Conceptual Skills</u> 3.   These skills involve the manager's ability to see the "big picture" of the organization as a whole and how each part contributes to its overall functioning, and are relatively important for top management.

Learning Goal 7.4
Explain the concept of leadership and identify the three basic leadership styles. (150-152)

---

1.   What is leadership?

132

2.   Describe the three basic styles of leadership.

3.   What helps determine which leadership style is "best"? Which leadership style are most businesses tending towards today?

Learning Goal 7.5
Describe the role of intrapreneurship in modern organizations. (152)

---

1.   What is intrapreneurship?

2.   Why are many corporations encouraging intrapreneurship?

Learning Goal 7.6

Explain the impact of downsizing and outsourcing on today's organizations. (142-144)

True or False

__T__ 1.   Downsizing refers to the elimination of layers of management in an effort to reduce costs and to make the firm more efficient.

__F__ 2.   Downsizing results in a " taller" organizational structure.

__T__ 3.   Reducing managerial layers requires two components in order to succeed: training and empowerment.

__F__ 4.   Empowerment means relying on outside specialists to perform functions previously performed by company employees.

__T__ 5.   Two important components of successful downsizing are employee empowerment and outsourcing.

__F__ 6.   Outsourcing means giving employees additional decision-making authority and responsibility.

Learning Goal 7.7

*List the steps in the decision-making process
and contrast programmed and nonprogrammed decisions.* (152-153)

1.   What are the five steps in the decision-making process?

134

2.   What is the difference between programmed and nonprogrammed decisions?

Learning Goal 7.8
Discuss the importance of time management. (153-154)

---

1.   Why is time management important to managers?

2.   What are some time management guidelines?

Name:_____ **Professor:**_____

Section:_____ **Date:**_____

SELF REVIEW

True or False

_____1.   Supervisory management is the highest level of management.

_____2.   Larger, more complex firms usually have a smaller number of levels of hierarchy.

_____3.   Departmentalization is designed to let individuals specialize in certain jobs and thus to become more efficient.

_____4.   Because an organizational chart specifies each area of an organization's responsibility and authority, it can help managers coordinate their activities.

_____5.   The line organizational structure is usually the best form for larger businesses.

_____6.   Most of today's business organizations combine elements of one or more types of organizational structures.

_____7.   The best type of leadership style depends on the leader, the followers, and the situation.

_____8.   The type of corporate culture has little impact on the success of the organization.

_____9.   Intrapreneurship is defined as the act of assigning activities to subordinates.

_____10.   Empowering employees means giving them additional decision-making authority and responsibility.

_____11.   Outsourcing refers to relying on outside specialists to perform functions previously performed by company employees.

_____12.   Nonprogrammed decisions involve simple, frequently occurring problems or opportunities for which solutions have been determined previously.

_____13.   Programmed decisions require considerable management involvement in identifying and evaluating alternatives.

_____14.   "Restructuring," the basic structural change occurring in corporations today, can be described as movement away from a "vertical" organizational structure toward a "horizontal" organizational structure.

136

Multiple Choice

1.   At any level of management, managers need the ability to:
     a.   lead and to motivate other people.
     b.   work in a team.
     c.   formulate and carry out long-range plans, and the courage to take risks.
     d.   relate to other people.
     e.   all of the above.

2.   Which of the following statements is true?
     a.   The functions performed by managers in accomplishing the goals of the organization include planning, organizing, leading, and controlling.
     b.   Organization can be defined as a structural grouping of people working together to achieve organizational objectives.
     c.   Organizing is the means by which management blends human and material resources by designing a formal structure of tasks and authority.
     d.   Three key elements are present in an organization: human interaction, goal-directed activities, and structure.
     e.   All of the above.

3.   Proctor & Gamble, manufacturers of such diverse products as potato chips, toothpaste, and laundry detergent, divides its organizational structure on the basis of the goods being produced. This is an example of:
     a.   process departmentalization.
     b.   functional departmentalization.
     c.   customer departmentalization.
     d.   product departmentalization.
     e.   geographic departmentalization.

4.   The matrix, or project management form of organizational structure is:
     a.   the simplest form of structure, but it suffers from a lack of specialization by management.
     b.   a structure in which specialists from different parts of the organization are brought together to work on specific projects.
     c.   a structure in which authority and responsibility are held jointly by a group of individuals rather than by a single manager.
     d.   based on a direct flow of authority form the chief executive to subordinates.
     e.   combines the direct flow of authority present in the line organization with staff departments that serve, advise, and support the line departments.

5.	The organizational approach which has been increasingly used by both medium-sized firms and large, multiproduct firms to focus diverse organizational resources on specific problems or projects is the:
	a.	line organizational structure.
	b.	line-and-staff organizational structure.
	c.	matrix organizational structure.
	d.	committee organizational structure.
	e.	leadership organizational structure.

6.	A manager who makes a decision on her own, communicates it to subordinates, and requires them to implement it, is exercising which of the following types of leadership styles?
	a.	Corporate leadership.
	b.	Autocratic leadership
	c.	Democratic leadership
	d.	Free-rein leadership.
	e.	Programmed leadership.

7.	Intrapreneurship:
	a.	is entrepreneurial-type activity within the corporate structure.
	b.	is the value system of an organization.
	c.	involves recognizing that a problem exists, identifying it, evaluating alternatives, selecting and implementing an alternative, and following up.
	d.	is an autocratic form of leadership.
	e.	is the effective allocation of one's time among different tasks.

8.	Outsourcing can complement downsizing by:
	a.	reducing the need for employees to perform certain tasks.
	b.	allowing a firm to specialize in what it does best.
	c.	allowing a firm to hire another company to undertake a task which it is more qualified to do.
	d.	allowing a firm to negotiate the best price from among a number of competing bidders.
	e.	all of the above.

138

9.   Which of the following statements is true concerning decision-making?
     a.   A systematic step-by-step approach to decision making is rarely effective for modern day managers.
     b.   Programmed decisions involve simple, frequently occurring problems or opportunities for which solutions have been determined previously.
     c.   Nonprogrammed decisions involve simple, frequently occurring problems or opportunities for which solutions have been determined previously.
     d.   Programmed decisions are decisions undertaken by computers.
     e.   All decisions should be made with quickly.

10. Time management:
     a.   is the scheduling of workers' hours.
     b.   is a minor ingredient to a manager's success.
     c.   begins with knowing what one's time is worth so that it can be allocated in a cost-effective manner.
     d.   rarely involves delegating work.
     e.   is a new level of organizational structure designed to monitor subordinates' time to complete a task.

11. Which of the following statements is true concerning the changing organizational structure of American corporations?
     a.   The old "vertical" structure was characterized by orders being passed down the chain of command and decisions being passed up, slowing the process.
     b.   The old "vertical" structure was characterized by work segmented according to functions, such as manufacturing , research, marketing, etc., with little overlap among highly specialized workers.
     c.   The new "horizontal" structure is characterized by workers being encouraged to make more decisions in an attempt to save time and money, and to respond better to the marketplace.
     d.   The new "horizontal" structure is characterized by specialized workers working together in groups on specific projects, cutting out layers of management.
     e.   All of the above.

Name:_____**Professor:**_____
Section:_____**Date:**_____

APPLICATION EXERCISES

1. What is the relationship between the form of organizational structure adopted by a firm and the style of leadership you would most likely observe? How might the "flatter," more "horizontal" organizational structures observed in corporations today accompanied by their more democratic styles of leadership be related?

2. Holding everything else the same, which type of leadership style do you think would be most appropriate in managing relatively unskilled workers? What about managing professionals?

140

3.   You are applying for a supervisory position in a local company. In preparing for the upcoming interview what types of managerial skills should you stress that you possess?

4.   You are at a party and one person comments that the downsizing taking place in corporate America is the result of greed on the part of corporations. Another person replies that because of the increased globalization of markets most of the downsizing is due to the increased competition facing American corporations from abroad. You are asked to respond. How do you reply?

5.   Why do firms establish "procedures," "policies," and "rules?"

Name:_____**Professor:**_____

Section:_____**Date:**_____

CROSSWORD PUZZLE

ACROSS

1. Entrepreneurial-type activity within the corporate culture.

3. The act of assigning activities to subordinates.

6. The achievement of organizational objectives through people and other resources.

9. Management decides to eliminate layers from the management hierarchy in an effort to reduce costs and make the firm more efficient.

DOWN

2. The highest level of the management hierarchy and is staffed by executives who develop long-range plans and interact with the public and outside entities, like the government. (2 words)

4. Giving employees additional decision-making authority and responsibility.

5. A structured grouping of people working together to achieve organizational objectives.

7. Act of motivating or causing others to perform activities designed to achieve specific objectives.

8. The effective allocation of one's time among different tasks. (2 words)

Junk
Chapter

CHAPTER 7 SOLUTIONS

Analysis of Learning Goals

Learning Goal 7.1
Fill in the Blank:
> Management
> Top management
> Middle management
> Supervisory management
> Supervisory management

Listing:
1.	First
2.	Third
3.	Fifth
4.	Second
5.	Fourth

Learning Goal 7.2
1. a		5. b
2. a		6. d
3. c		7. c
4. d		8. b

Learning Goal 7.3
1. Technical skills
2. Human relation skills
3. Conceptual skills

Learning Goal 7.4
1. Leadership is the act of motivating or causing others to perform activities designed to achieve specific objectives.

2. The three basic styles of leadership are autocratic, democratic, and free-rein. The autocratic leader makes a decision on her own without consulting others. Democratic leaders involve subordinates in making decisions. Free-rein leaders believe in minimal supervision and leave most decisions to their subordinates.

3. The best type of leadership style depends on three elements: the leader, the followers, and the situation. Today, the general trend is toward greater participation of subordinates in decisions that affect them.

144

Learning Goal 7.5
1. Intrapreneurship refers to various attempts to make large organizations more entrepreneurial.

2. Intrapreneurship within corporations is encouraged because intrapreneurship units achieve the innovation dynamics of a smaller firm. These units are given free rein (and sometimes financial incentives it accomplish their assigned objectives.

Learning Goal 7.6

1.	True	4.	False
2.	False	5.	True
3.	True	6.	False

Learning Goal 7.7
1. The five steps in the decision-making process are:
    1. Recognition of problems and opportunities.
    2. Development of alternative courses.
    3. Evaluation of alternatives.
    4. Selection and implementation of the chosen alternative.
    5. Follow up to determine the effectiveness of decisions.

2. Programmed decisions involve simple, frequently occurring problems or opportunities for which solutions have been determined previously. Such decisions are make quickly by reference to a rule or procedure, and managers need spend little time in identifying and evaluating alternatives.
    By contrast, nonprogrammed decisions involve more complex, relatively unique situations. Their solution requires considerable management involvement in identifying and evaluating alternatives.

Learning Goal 7.8
1. Time management refers to the process of allocating one's time among different activities. Given the variety of goals management is expected to accomplish in a limited amount of time, it has become evident in recent years that time management is a major ingredient in managerial success.

2. The starting point in effective time management is to know what one's time is worth so that it can be allocated in a cost-effective manner. Additional guidelines include: a) establish goals and set priorities; b) learn to delegate work; c)concentrate on most important activities; d) do most important work when most alert. e) group activities together; and f) learn to handle interruptions.

Self-Review

True or False

1.	F	4.	T	7.	T	10.	T	13.	F
2.	F	5.	F	8.	F	11.	T	14.	T
3.	T	6.	T	9.	F	12.	F		

Multiple Choice

1.	e	4.	b	7.	a	10.	c
2.	e	5.	c	8.	e	11.	e
3.	d	6.	b	9.	b		

Application Exercises

1. In the line organization, in which decisions are passed down from the top to ever lower levels of management one would likely find a more authoritarian style of leadership displayed. (If it helps, you may think of this as the "military" form of organization and style of leadership.) In a matrix organizational structure where specialists from different departments (with different immediate supervisors) within the firm come together to work on a project or problem one would likely observe a more democratic style of leadership.

    The "flatter," more "horizontal" structures of many corporations today, where many middle management positions have been eliminated, requires more direct communication, cooperation and input from employees. A more democratic form of leadership is more fruitful in empowering employees with greater responsibility and input into the decision-making process. Moreover, when people believe they have had an input into the decision-making process they will more likely see to its success.

2. Unskilled workers are typically less sophisticated and motivated. A more authoritarian style of leadership may prove to be most fruitful in "getting the job done." However, most professionals don't take too kindly to "being bossed around." A more democratic, or free-rein leadership style is usually more appropriate and successful.

3. Although the three basic managerial skills---technical, human relations, and conceptual----necessary for effective management are important at all levels of management, technical skills are relatively more important at the supervisory level. But because human relation skills are equally important at all levels of management, then you should stress your technical *and* human relation skills in the interview.

4. It may be true that some corporations are concentrating too much on short-run profit-maximization and are therefore looking for any way to reduce costs by downsizing (even though long-term thinking may question this wisdom). However, it is also true that there

146

is increased competition facing corporate America from abroad. This greater competition has forced American corporations to look for more effective ways to organize, to reduce their costs, to increase their price competitiveness in the global economy. The greater competition from abroad forcing American firms to seek out more cost-effective means of production will not likely go away. Whether downsizing your staff is appropriate to achieve a competitive advantage is debatable.

5.　　"Rules," policies," and "procedures" are really programmed decisions. These types of decisions involve simple, frequently occurring problems or opportunities for which solutions have been determined previously. Such decisions are made quickly by making reference to a rule, procedure, or company policy, and managers need spend little time in identifying and evaluating alternatives. In sum, rules and procedures allow managers to spend their time more wisely on more important matters. They are a form of built-in time management tool for managers.

Crossword Puzzle

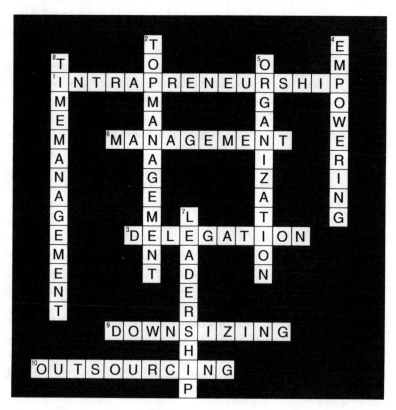

CHAPTER 7

Chapter 8

The Human Resource

"The importance of people to the success of any organization is stressed in the very definition of 'management': the use of people and other resources in accomplishing organizational objectives." (162)

KEY CONCEPTS

Human resource management	Process of acquiring, training, developing, motivating, and appraising a sufficient quantity of qualified employees to perform necessary activities; and developing activities and an organizational climate conducive to maximum efficiency and worker satisfaction. (162)
Morale	The mental attitude of employees toward their employer and job. (163)
Need	The lack of something useful. (164)
Motive	The inner state that directs us toward the goal of satisfying a felt need. (164)
Theory X	Assumes that employees dislike work and must be coerced, controlled, or threatened to motivate them to work. (166)
Theory Y	An assumption that workers like work and, under proper conditions, accept and seek out responsibilities to fulfill their social, esteem and self-actualization needs. (166)
Theory Z	Views involved workers as the key to increased productivity for the company and an improved quality of work life for the employee. (166)
On-the-job training	Employees are trained for job tasks by allowing them to perform them under the guidance of an experienced employee. (168)
Management-development program	Training designed to improve the skills and broaden the knowledge of current and potential managers. (168)

148

Performance appraisals	The evaluation of an individual's job performance by comparing actual performance with desired performance. (168)
Employee benefits	Rewards such as pension plans, insurance, sick leave, child care, and tuition reimbursement given at all or part of the expense of the company. (169)
Job enrichment	Redesigning work to give employees more authority in planning their tasks, deciding how the work is to be done, and allowing them to learn related skills or trade jobs with others. (170)
Flextime	A work-scheduling system that allows employees to set work hours within constraints specified by the firm. (172)
Home-based work	Working the same jobs, but doing the work at home instead of in the office. (172)
Labor union	A group of workers who have banded together to achieve common goals in the key areas of wages, hours, and working conditions. (173)
Collective bargaining	A process of negotiation between management and union representatives for the purpose of arriving at mutually acceptable wages and working conditions for employees. (173)
Mediation	The process of settling union-management disputes through recommendations of an impartial third party. (175)
Arbitration	Bringing in an impartial third party, called an arbitrator, who renders a legally binding decision. (175)
Worker buyout plans	Financial incentives to encourage voluntary retirement. (177)
Glass ceiling	An invisible barrier difficult for women and minorities to pass. (178)

Name:_____**Professor:**_____

Section:_____**Date:**_____

ANALYSIS OF LEARNING GOALS

Learning Goal 8.1

Explain the importance of human resource management and the responsibilities of a human resource department. (162-164)

---

1.   What is human resource management?

2.   Why is human resource management becoming increasingly important?

3.   What are the responsibilities of a human resource department?

150

Learning Goal 8.2
List the different needs in Maslow's hierarchy. (164-166)

Matching

Match the five following hierarchy of needs according to Maslow with the statements below.

a.	Physiological needs	d.	Esteem needs
b.	Safety needs	e.	Self-actualization needs
c.	Social (belongingness) needs		

_D_ 1.   Recognition, approval of others, status, increased responsibilities.

_A_ 2.   Food, water, and shelter.

C _3._   Acceptance, affection, affiliation with work groups, family, friends, coworkers, and supervisors.

B _4._   Protection form harm, employee benefits, job security.

_E_ 5.   Accomplishment, opportunities for advancement, growth, and creativity.

Learning Goal 8.3
Distinguish between Theory X, Theory Y, and Theory Z managers. (166-167)

Fill in the Blank

The traditional _____X_____ manager views workers as being lazy, disliking work, and requiring close and constant supervision. _____Y_____ assumes employees want to satisfy social, esteem, and self-actualization needs through work as well as through other activities. They emphasize employee self control and self direction. A

_____Z_____ organization is more likely to include long-term employment, shared decision making, relatively slow promotions and evaluations, and varied and nonspecialized job assignments. The _____Z_____ approach emphasizes involved workers as the key to increased productivity and improved quality of work life.

Learning Goal 8.4

Explain how recruitment, selection, orientation, training, and evaluation contribute to placing the right person in the job. (167-169)

---

1.   List the steps in the recruitment and selection process.

2.   What role does training and evaluation have in the work place?

Learning Goal 8.5

Explain the concept of job enrichment and how it can motivate employees. (170-171)

True or False

__T__ 1.   Job enrichment involves redesigning work to give employees more authority in planning their tasks, deciding how the work is to be done, and allowing them to learn related skills or trade jobs with others.

__F__ 2.   Job enlargement is where employees work the same number of hours in fewer than the typical five days.

__T__ 3.   Flextime is a work-scheduling system that allows employees to set work hours within constraints specified by the firm.

152

F 4.   A compressed workweek is the division of one job assignment between two or
         more employees.

F 5.   Job sharing sometimes is used interchangeably with job enrichment, but it
         differs in that it is merely an expansion of a worker's assignment to include
         additional, but smaller, tasks.

T 6.   Home-based work is working the same jobs, but doing the work at home
         instead of in the office.

Learning Goal 8.6
Outline the different forms of compensation. (169-170)

---

1.   The compensation policy of most companies is based on five factors. What are they?

2.   There are four types of incentive compensation designed to reward exceptional
      performance by the individual. List the type being described by each of the following
      statements.

      a. _Profit-Sharing_ Bonus based on company profits.

      b. _Lump-Sum Bonus_ One-time cash payment based on performance.

      c. _Pay for Knowledge_ Salary increase based on learning new job tasks.

      d. _Gain Sharing_ Bonus based on surpassing predetermined performance
         goals.

Learning Goal 8.7
Summarize the role of labor unions and list their primary goals. (173-175)

1.   Describe the role of labor unions and list their primary goals.

2.   What contributions have unions made to the business environment?

Learning Goal 8.8
Outline the sources of power, or "weapons," of labor and management. (175-177)

True or False

T   1.   A strike is a walkout, or temporary work stoppage by employees.

F   2.   Picketing is an organized attempt to keep the public form purchasing the goods or services of a firm

F   3.   A boycott occurs when workers march at the entrance of the employer's plant as a public protest against some management practice.

T   4.   A lockout is, in essence, a management strike because management closes the firm.

T   5.   Strikebreakers are nonunion workers who cross picket lines to fill the jobs of striking workers.

F   6.   An injunction is a cooperative effort by employers to all agree not to succumb to union demands.

Learning Goal 8.9
*Identify and briefly describe each of the major human resource concerns
for the twenty-first century.* (177-179)

Describe

Identify and briefly describe each of the major human resource concerns for the twenty-first
century.

Name:_____ **Professor:**_____

Section:_____ **Date:**_____

SELF REVIEW

True or False

___T___ 1.　The three "Rs" which should contribute to higher employee morale are worker responsibility, rewards, and rights.

___T___ 2.　Effective management of people results from an understanding of human needs and the ability of the organization to make satisfying individual needs consistent with organizational goals.

___T___ 3.　A satisfied need is no longer a motivator.

___F___ 4.　Theory X managers consider the expenditure of physical and mental effort by workers as natural as play or rest.

___T___ 5.　Theory Z organizations blend Theory Y assumptions with Japanese management practices.

___F___ 6.　On-the-job training is designed to improve the skills and broaden the knowledge of current and potential managers.

___T___ 7.　Employee training should be viewed as an ongoing process.

___F___ 8.　Flextime is where employees work the same number of hours in fewer than the typical five days.

___T___ 9.　Employee benefits are a large and growing component of human resource costs.

___T___ 10.　The *Family and Medical Leave Act of 1993* requires covered employees to give up to 12 weeks of unpaid, job-protected leave to eligible employees.

___F___ 11.　A lockout is a temporary work stoppage brought about by employees.

___F___ 12.　A strike is an organized attempt to keep the public from purchasing goods or services of a firm.

___T___ 13.　A worker buyout plan involves a financial incentive to encourage voluntary retirement.

___T___ 14.　The glass ceiling is an invisible barrier difficult for women and minorities to pass.

156

Multiple Choice

1. The objectives of a human resource department include:
    a. providing qualified, well-trained employees.
    b. maximizing employee effectiveness in the organization.
    c. satisfying individual employee needs through monetary compensation, employee benefits, advancement opportunities, and job satisfaction.
    d. all of the above.
    e. none of the above.

2. According to Maslow's hierarchy of human needs:
    a. People are wanting animals whose needs depend on what they already possess.
    b. a satisfied need is not a motivator; only those needs that have not been satisfied can influence behavior.
    c. people's needs are arranged in a hierarchy of importance.
    d. once one need has been partially satisfied, another emerges and demands satisfaction.
    e. all of the above.

3. According to Maslow's hierarchy of needs the highest order needs are:
    a. self-actualization needs.
    b. esteem needs.
    c. social needs.
    d. safety needs.
    e. physiological needs.

4. Managers who believe that the average person prefers to be directed, wishes to avoid responsibility, has relatively little ambition, and wants security above all will most likely undertake management according to:
    a. Theory A
    b. Theory Z
    c. Theory X
    d. Theory Y
    e. Theory C

5. Job enrichment refers to:
    a. employees who are trained for job tasks by allowing them to perform them under the guidance of an experienced employee.
    b. redesigning work to give employees more authority in planning their tasks, deciding how the work is to be done, and allowing them to learn related skills or trade jobs with others.
    c. the evaluation of an individual's job performance by comparing actual performance with desired performance.
    d. training designed to improve the skills and broaden the knowledge of current and potential managers.
    e. rewards such as pension plans, insurance, sick leave, child care, and tuition reimbursement.

6. Redesigning work to give employees more authority in planning their tasks, deciding how the work is to be done, and allowing them to learn related skills or trade jobs with others is known as:
    a. job enrichment.
    b. job enlargement.
    c. flextime.
    d. a compressed workweek.
    e. home-based work.

7. A company's compensation policy is based on:
    a. salaries and wages paid by other companies in the area that compete for the same personnel.
    b. government legislation
    c. the cost of living.
    d. the ability of the company to pay, and the worker's productivity.
    e. all of the above.

8. Profit sharing is:
    a. a bonus based on company profits.
    b. a one-time cash payment based on performance.
    c. a salary increase based on learning new job tasks.
    d. a bonus based on surpassing predetermined performance goals.
    e. any of the above.

158

9. Which of the following statements is true?
    a. A labor union is a political party interested in promoting socialist political policies.
    b. Collective bargaining is the negotiating process between management and union representatives for the purpose of arriving at a mutually acceptable wage and working conditions for employees.
    c. Arbitration is the process of settling union-management disputes through recommendations of an impartial third party.
    d. Mediation is the bringing in of an impartial third party, called an arbitrator, who renders a legally binding decision between the union and management.
    e. A grievance is a binding union contract.

10. Which of the following statements are true concerning disputes between labor and management?
    a. The chief weapons of unions are the strikebreakers, injunctions, lockouts, and employer's associations.
    b. The chief weapons of management are the strike, picketing, and boycotts.
    c. Most differences between labor and management ar settled through the collective bargaining process or through formal grievance procedures.
    d. Strikes are now illegal.
    e. All of the above.

11. Which of the following is a challenge facing human resource management in the next century?
    a. Finding cost effective ways to retain valuable older workers.
    b. Meeting the needs of two-career households.
    c. Breaking through the glass ceiling and managing a culturally diverse work force.
    d. The growth in part-time employees.
    e. All of the above.

Name:_____**Professor:**_____
Section:_____**Date:**_____

APPLICATION EXERCISES

1. "Right to work" laws have been passed in many states. A right to work law enables an employee to be hired by a company without having to join the union as a condition of continued employment. What impact do you think the passage of right to work laws have had on the declining membership within unions?

2. What are the benefits and the costs of hiring from within the company? What about filling a position by hiring from outside the firm?

160

3. Some managers of production facilities in less developed foreign countries with less aggressive work ethics have found it challenging to motivate their workers. From what you have read in this chapter what would you propose?

Name:_____ **Professor:**_____

Section:_____**Date:**_____

ACROSS

1 . Rewards such as pension plans, insurance, sick leave, child care, and tuition reimbursement given at all or part of the expense of the company. (2 words)

3. The process of settling union-management disputes through recommendations of an impartial third party.

9. A group of workers who have banded together to achieve common goals in the key areas of wages, hours, and working conditions. (2 words)

DOWN

2. A work-scheduling system that allows employees to set work hours within constraints specified by the firm.

4. The lack of something useful.

5. Employees are trained for job tasks by allowing them to perform them under the guidance of an experienced employee. (4 words)

6. The inner state that directs us toward the goal of satisfying need.

7. The mental attitude of employees toward their employer and job.

8. Bringing in an impartial third party, called an arbitrator, who renders a legally binding decision.

Job Enlargement = add more of same tasks and duties to job

Job Enrichment = add authority, responsibility, & opportunity for decision making to do.

Union
strike
Picketing
Boycott

Managerial
strike breakers
Lockout
Injunction
Employer Associations

CHAPTER 8 SOLUTIONS

Analysis of Learning Goals

Learning Goal 6.1
1.   Human resource management is the process of acquiring, training, developing, motivating, and appraising a sufficient quantity of qualified employees to perform necessary activities; and developing activities and an organizational climate conducive to maximum efficiency and worker satisfaction.

2.   Human resource management is becoming increasingly important because of increased competition, growth in the use of outsourcing and part-time workers, a new emphasis on cost control, complex wage and benefit programs, and a changing work force.

3.   A human resource management department is responsible for handling human resource planning, developing job descriptions and job specifications, screening job applicants, developing and administering testing programs, interviewing new employees, and administering compensation, benefits, and safety programs.

Learning Goal 6.2
1. d   2. a   3. c   4. b   5. e

Learning Goal 6.3
Theory X
Theory Y
Theory Z
Theory Z

Learning Goal 6.4
1.   The steps involved in the recruitment and selection process (rejection may occur at any of these steps) include:
     1.   Initial contact with job applicants.
     2.   Application form.
     3.   Employment tests.
     4.   Interviews by human resource department and supervisor.
     5.   Background checks..
     6.   Medical examination.

2.   Once an employee is hired and has gone through orientation, then a major function of the human resource department is developing and maintaining a well-trained, productive

164

labor force. Employee training should be viewed as an ongoing process throughout an employee's tenure with the company On-the-job training is designed to upgrade the skills of an employee. Management-development programs are designed for managers.

Evaluation is the process of comparing actual performance against desired performance to make objective decisions about compensation, promotion, additional training needs, transfers, or termination.

Learning Goal 6.5

1. True	4. False
2. False	5. False
3. True	6. True

Learning Goal 6.6

1.   The five factors which determine a company's compensation policy are:
   1.   Salaries and wages paid by other companies in the area that compete for the same personnel.
   2.   Government legislation
   3.   The cost of living.
   4.   The ability of the company to pay.
   5.   The worker's productivity.

2.   a. Profit-sharing
        b. Lump-sum bonus
        c. Pay for knowledge
        d. Gain sharing

Learning Goal 6.7

1.   Labor unions are designed to protect the interests of employees in the key areas of wages, hours, and working conditions.

2.   Union influence has helped to achieve many innovations in business, such as the standard 40-hour workweek, safer working conditions, a guaranteed minimum wage, and the presence of employee-designated members on corporate boards of directors.

Learning Goal 6.8

1. True	4. True
2. False	5. True
3. False	6. False

Learning Goal 6.9
Current issues in human resource management include:
1. Finding cost-effective ways to retain valuable older workers.
2. Meeting the needs of two-career households.
3. Breaking through the glass ceiling.
4. The growth in part-time employees as a result of automation and downsizing.
5. Managing a culturally diverse work force.

Self-Review

True or False
1. T	4. F	7. T	10. T	13. T
2. T	5. T	8. F	11. F	14. T
3. T	6. F	9. T	12. F	

Multiple Choice
1. d	4. c	7. e	10. c
2. e	5. b	8. a	11. e
3. a	6. a	9. b	

Application Exercises

1. It is difficult to say exactly what the impact of the passage of right to work laws have had on union membership. However, the opponents of right to work laws argue that because management, generally speaking, is not too interested in hiring someone whom may join the union, then it may put applicants in the uncomfortable position of giving the impression they are not too fond of unions in order to get the job. This puts pressure on workers not to join the union later because doing so may be viewed negatively by management reducing any chances at promotion. In sum, the presence of right to work laws may, in practice, result in a decline in union membership and union influence in protecting worker's interests.

2. A benefit of hiring from within the company is that the employee is already familiar with the organization and its culture. Another benefit is that it rewards hard work by reminding people that promotions are a realistic possibility. Some of the costs of hiring from within include the loss of an opportunity to "bring in new blood," and it may create some undesired animosity by those employees not chosen to fill the position. The benefits and costs of hiring from outside the company are the converse of those for hiring from within. That is, hiring from outside provides an opportunity to bring in new ideas and it precludes the necessity of having to chose from many current qualified employees. The costs include having to assimilate the new employee into the company.

166

3.   According to Maslow's theory a satisfied need is not a motivator. Therefore, it may be helpful to try to get the employees to find new needs. Inasmuch as a manager is successful in stimulating these new needs and indicating how hard work within the company will satisfy those new needs then all the better. It is interesting to note that some managers introduced magazines in workers' lounges featuring new modern consumer durable and nondurable goods and services (e.g. washing machines, stereos, etc...) designed to wet the appetite for these items. It worked. Employees started working harder to obtain these items.

Crossword Puzzle

CHAPTER 8

Chapter 9
Teamwork and Communication

"Teamwork...[is] one of the major business opportunities and challenges of the late 1990s." (186)

KEY CONCEPTS

Team	A small number of people with complementary skills who are committed to a common purpose, approach, and set of performance goals. (186)
Work teams	A mid-1990s approach in which small numbers of people with complementary skills perform the day-to-day work of the organization. (188)
Problem-solving teams	Temporary combinations of workers who gather to solve a specific problem and then disband. (188)
Task specialist role	The role of devoting time and energy to helping the team accomplish its goals. (189)
Socio-emotional role	The role of devoting time and energy to providing support for group members' emotional needs and social unity. (189)
Team cohesiveness	The extent to which team members are attracted to the team and motivated to remain a part of it. (192)
Team norm	A standard of conduct that is shared by team members and guides their behavior. (192)
Conflict	Antagonistic interaction in which one party attempts to thwart the intentions or goals of another. (193)
Communication	The meaningful exchange of information through messages. (195)

168

Listening	The skill of receiving a message and interpreting its genuine meaning by accurately grasping the facts and feelings conveyed. (196)
Formal communication channels	Messages that flow within the chain of command or task responsibility defined by an organization. (197)
Informal communication channels	Communication that exists outside formally authorized channels without regard for the organization's hierarchy of authority. (198)
Grapevine	An internal information channel that conducts information through unofficial, independent sources. (198)
Nonverbal communication	Communication that is transmitted through actions and behaviors. (198)
Internal communication	Communication through channels within an organization. (199)
Centralized network	Team members communicate through a single person to solve problems or make decisions. (200)
Decentralized network	Members communicate freely with other team members and arrive at decisions together. (200)
External communication	The meaningful exchange of information through messages between an organization and its major audiences. (202)
Low-context cultures	Communication which tends to rely on written and verbal messages. (204)
High-context cultures	Communication which tends to rely not only on the message itself, but also on everything that surrounds it. (204)

Name:_____**Professor:**_____
Section:_____**Date:**_____

ANALYSIS OF LEARNING GOALS

Learning Goal 9.1

Distinguish between the two major types of teams found in organizations. (187-188)

Multiple Choice

1. Which of the following is *not* one the five general types of teams?
    a. Problem-solving teams.
    b. Work teams.
    c. Quality circles.
    d. Softball teams.

2. Teams:
    a. usually have more than 15 members.
    b. have members who have different goals if the team is to be effective.
    c. have members who hold themselves mutually responsible and accountable for accomplishing their objectives.
    d. all of the above.

3. Work teams:
    a. are used by about two-thirds of U.S. companies.
    b. that are empowered with the authority to make decisions about how the work gets done, are properly described as self-managed teams.
    c. consist of small numbers of people with complementary skills who perform the day-to-day work of the organization.
    d. all of the above.

4. Problem-solving teams:
    a. and management teams are the two major types of teams found in organizations.
    b. are different from quality circles because problem-solving teams are permanent committees designed to handle whatever work-place problems which may arise.
    c. are different from quality circles because problem-solving teams have specific missions that are always narrow in focus.
    d. usually disband once the task has been completed.

170

Learning Goal 9.2
*Identify the characteristics of an effective team and the different roles
played by team members.* (188-190)

True or False

____T____ 1.   Effective teams have between 5 and 12 members, with about 7 members being the ideal size. T

____T____ 2.   Research indicates that diverse teams tend to display a broader range of viewpoints and produce more innovative solutions to problems. T

____F____ 3.   The team member who assumes the role as task specialist is one who devotes time and energy to encourage team harmony. T

____T____ 4.   The team member who assumes a nonparticipative role makes minimal contributions to either tasks or team members' socio-emotional needs. T

____F____ 5.   Team members who play a socio-emotional role devote time and energy to accomplishing team goals. f

____F____ 6.   Team members who assume a "dual" role are team members who make minimal contributions to either tasks or team members' socio-emotional needs.

Learning Goal 9.3
Summarize the stages of team development. (190-192)

Matching
Match the following stages of team development with the statements that follow.

a.   forming   d.   performing
b.   storming   e.   adjourning
c.   norming

____C____ 1.   When differences are resolved, members accept each other, and consensus is reached about the roles of the team leader and other participants.

____A____ 2.   An orientation period during which team members get to know each other and find out what behaviors are acceptable to the group.

B _ 3.   The stage in which individual personalities emerge as they clarify their roles and expectations.

E _ 4.   The focus is on wrapping up and summarizing the team's experience and accomplishments.

D _ 5.   This stage is characterized by problem solving and a focus on task accomplishment.

Learning Goal 9.4
Relate team cohesiveness and norms to effective team performance. (192)

Describe

Describe how team cohesiveness and norms are related to team performance.

Learning Goal 9.5
Describe the factors that can cause conflict in teams,
and discuss conflict resolution styles. (193-195)

---

1.   What are the sources of conflict in teams?

172

2.　　What are the different conflict resolution styles? Which is the most effective? What can a team leader do to reduce conflict?

Learning Goal 9.6
Explain the importance of effective communication skills in business. (195)

1.　　Explain the importance of effective communication skills in business.

2.　　Every communication follows a step-by-step process that can be thought of as an interaction among six elements. What are those six elements?

Learning Goal 9.7
Compare the different types of communication. (195-204)

Listing

List the different forms of communication described by the following statements.

Non-verbal   1.   Communication transmitted through actions and behaviors rather than through words.

Verbal   2.   Transmission of messages in the form of words.

Informal   3.   Communication transmitted outside formally authorized channels without regard for the organization's hierarchy of authority.

Oral   4.   Communication transmitted through speech.

Written   5.   Communication transmitted through writing.

Formal   6.   Communication transmitted through the chain of command within an organization to other members or to persons outside the organization.

Multiple Choice

7.   It is convenient to discuss communication based on the following forms:
   - a.   oral and written.
   - b.   formal and informal.
   - c.   verbal and nonverbal.
   - d.   all of the above.

8.   Active listening is:
   - a.   defensive listening that occurs when recipients of a message feel its goal is to take advantage of them.
   - b.   listening to catch the speaker in a mistake or contradiction.
   - c.   mechanical listening done to be polite rather than to communicate.
   - d.   a form of listening that requires involvement with the information and empathy with the speaker's situation.

174

9. A grapevine is:
    a. a formal channel of communication.
    b. a form of communication through unofficial, independent sources.
    c. a form of nonverbal communication.
    d. the term describing the uncomfortable feeling when a person invades your body zone.

10. Which of the following statements is true?
    a. Internal communication is a message made to customers of a firm.
    b. In a centralized network of communication in teams, team members communicate through a single person to solve problems or make decisions.
    c. When members communicate freely with other team members and arrive at decisions together then the team is practicing a centralized network of communication.
    d. Generally, when verbal and nonverbal cues conflict, the receivers of the communication tend to believe the verbal elements.

Learning Goal 9.8

Identify and explain several important considerations in international business communications. (204-205)

Describe

Identify and explain several important considerations in international business communications.

Learning Goal 9.9

Summarize important developments in communication technology and how they affect business communication. (205)

Describe

Summarize important developments in communication technology and how they affect business communication.

Name:_____ **Professor:**_____

Section:_____ **Date:**_____

SELF REVIEW

True or False

___F___ 1.   Problem-solving teams are a small number of people with complementary skills who perform the day-to-day work of the organization.

___T___ 2.   A cross-functional team can either be a work team or a problem-solving team.

___T___ 3.   Teams are capable of increasing productivity, raising morale, and nurturing innovation.

___T___ 4.   Ideally, teams will contain a balance of members who play the task specialist, socio-emotional, and dual roles.

___F___ 5.   All companies should organize their employees as teams.

___F___ 6.   When team cohesiveness is low, productivity of team members and therefore team performance increases.

___T___ 7.   The avoiding style of conflict resolution is most effective when the cause of conflict is trivial or a no-win situation, when more information is needed, or when open conflict would be harmful

___T___ 8.   Active listening is the basis for effective communication.

___T___ 9.   Effective written communication reflects its audience, the channel being used, and the degree of formality that is appropriate.

___F___ 10.   An example of formal communication would be rumors spread through the grapevine.

___F___ 11.   Nonverbal communication is rarely as important as verbal communication.

___T___ 12.   Communication in low-context cultures tends to rely on explicit written and verbal messages.

___F___ 13.   The United States is an example of a high-context culture.

___T___ 14.   The ability to communicate cross-culturally is becoming increasingly important in business.

178

Multiple Choice

1. The two major types of teams found in organizations are:
    a. Problem-solving teams and work teams.
    b. Quality circles and virtual teams.
    c. Management teams and problem-solving teams.
    d. Virtual teams and work teams.
    e. Virtual teams and quality circles.

2. Work teams:
    a. usually have less than 15 members.
    b. have a common goal and all team members work to achieve it.
    c. have members who hold themselves mutually responsible and accountable for accomplishing their objectives.
    d. consist of a small number of people with complementary skills who perform the day-to-day work of the organization.
    e. all of the above.

3. Problem-solving teams:
    a. consist of a small number of people with complementary skills who perform the day-to-day work of the organization.
    b. are temporary combinations of workers who gather to solve a specific problem and then disband.
    c. are the same as quality circles.
    d. meet intermittently to air work-place problems.
    e. are the least popular type of team effort in business today.

4. Which of the following statements is true about the characteristics of an effective team and the different roles played by team members?
    a. Three important characteristics of teams are their size, the roles played by team members, and their diversity.
    b. Effective teams have between 5 and 12 members, with about 7 members being the ideal size.
    c. The team member who assumes a task specialist role devotes time and energy to helping the team accomplish its goals, whereas the socio-emotional role devotes time and energy to providing support for the group members' emotional needs and social unity.
    d. Research indicates that diverse teams tend to display a broader range of viewpoints and produce more innovative solutions to problems.
    e. All of the above.

5.   The performing stage of team development is characterized by:
     a.   problem solving and a focus on task accomplishment.
     b.   team members getting to know each other and finding out what behaviors are acceptable to the group.
     c.   individual personalities emerging as roles and expectations are clarified.
     d.   wrapping up and summarizing the team's experience and accomplishments.
     e.   members resolving differences, members learning to accept each other, and consensus is reached about the roles of the team leader and other participants.

6.   Which of the following will most likely increase team performance?
     a.   Highly cohesive teams.
     b.   A lack of a team norm.
     c.   A low level of diversity among team members.
     d.   Workers are not empowered.
     e.   Team members assume nonparticipative roles.

7.   The collaborating style of conflict resolution by a team leader is characterized by:
     a.   a decisive assertive approach.
     b.   neither being assertive nor cooperative.
     c.   a moderate degree of both assertiveness and cooperativeness.
     d.   a high degree of both assertiveness and cooperativeness.
     e.   a high degree of cooperativeness.

8.   Which of the following statement is true concerning communication?
     a.   Generally, when verbal and nonverbal cues conflict, the receivers of the communication tend to believe the nonverbal elements.
     b.   Managers spend 80 percent of their time in direct communication with others, and the other 20 percent on desk work, much of which is also communication in the form of writing and reading.
     c.   Communicators need to pay attention to audience feedback, even solicit it.
     d.   While some people feel oral channels allow them to convey their message more accurately, nonverbal cues can distort it.
     e.   All of the above.

180

9.   Which of the following statement is true concerning communication?
    a.   Nonverbal communication plays a much smaller role in communicating than most people think.
    b.   Examples of internal formal communication would include memos, reports, meetings, written proposals, oral presentations and meeting minutes.
    c.   "Polite listening" allows for the most effective communication.
    d.   A centralized communication network within a team is always the most effective type of communication within a team.
    e.   All of the above.

10.   International business communication:
    a.   has become more difficult with the development of new communication technologies.
    b.   in high-context cultures tends to rely on explicit written and verbal messages.
    c.   in low-context cultures is more likely to depend not only on the message itself, but also on everything that surrounds it.
    d.   requires American businesspeople to be less direct and more patient when doing business in more high-context cultures.
    e.   all of the above.

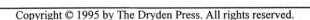

Name:_____Professor:_____

Section:_____Date:_____

APPLICATION EXERCISES

1.   Which type of conflict resolution do you think would be most appropriate in each of the following situations? Why?

      a.   One "prepy" team member complains of another's lack of taste in the latest fashion wear.

      b.   The company is forced to reduce everyone's wages by 10 percent if it wishes to remain in business.

      c.   One team member from the marketing department complains about how slow a new product is being developed. She fears that competing firms may introduce to the market a similar product sooner. This could result in a loss of substantial profits. Another equally well respected team member, from the engineering department, argues that moving too quickly through the development stage could result in a less than high-quality product being produced, thereby hurting long-run sales and profitability.

182

d.   A team is put together from various departments within the organization to develop a new product that is not expected by upper management to be introduced to the market for quite some time. This cross-functional team is starting from scratch with little information about consumer needs, etc. A wide variety of personalities comprise the team. An unmarried, "work-aholic" team member wants to start working on Saturdays right away to more quickly bring this problem-solving team to closure. Other team members don't believe that it is necessary to move so quickly. One team member believed to be a spokesperson for the group mutters that the "work-aholic" is a little over-ambitious for promotion.

e.   The union is demanding more benefit coverage in the union contract to cover the increasing cost of health care premiums. The company is concerned about the increasing costs associated with its labor force.

2.   What can a team leader do to reduce team conflict?

3.   How important do you think it is for a manager to be a "good listener." What type of listening behavior would be most appropriate? Why?

4.   What are the advantages of a cross-functional team?

Name:_____ **Professor:**_____
Section:_____ **Date:**_____

ACROSS

1. Team members communicate through a single person to solve problems or make decisions. (2 words)

3. The skill of receiving a message and interpreting its genuine meaning by accurately grasping the facts and feelings conveyed.

5. A standard of conduct that is shared by team members and guides their behavior. (2 words)

7. A small number of people with complementary skills who are committed to a common purpose, approach, and set of performance goals.

8. Antagonistic interaction in which one party attempts to thwart the intentions or goals of another.

10. The type of communication channels in which messages flow within the chain of command or task responsibility defined by an organization.

DOWN

2. A mid-1990s approach in which small numbers of people with complementary skills perform the day-to-day work of the organization. (2 words)

4. An internal information channel that conducts information through unofficial, independent sources.

6. The meaningful exchange of information through messages.

9. The type of communication that occurs through channels within an organization.

11. The type of communication channels that exist outside formally authorized channels without regard for the organization's hierarchy of authority.

12. The type of communication that is transmitted through actions and behaviors.

CHAPTER 9 SOLUTIONS

Analysis of Learning Goals

Learning Goal 9.1
1. d   2. c   3. d   4. d

Learning Goal 9.2
1. True
2. True
3. False
4. True
5. False
6. False

Learning Goal 9.3
1. c   2. a   3. b   4. e   5. d

Learning Goal 9.4
     Team cohesiveness is the extent to which team members are attracted to the team and motivated to remain a part of it. This cohesiveness typically increases when members interact frequently, share common attitudes and goals, and enjoy being together. When cohesiveness is low, morale suffers and team performance falls.

     A team norm is a standard of conduct that is shared by team members and guides their behavior. Team norms conducive to cooperation will enhance team performance.

Learning Goal 9.5
1. Conflict can stem from many sources: competition for scarce resources, personality clashes, conflicting goals, poor communication, unclear job responsibilities or team role assignments.

2. Conflict resolution styles cover a continuum, from assertive to cooperative. The most effective resolution style varies according to the situation. Resolution styles include: the competing style, the avoiding style, the compromising style, the accommodating style, and the collaborating style. A team leader can reduce conflict by focusing team members on broad goals, clarifying participants' respective tasks and areas of authority, acting as a mediator, and facilitating effective communication.

188

Learning Goal 9.6
1.   Communication can be defined as the meaningful exchange of information through messages, and it is essential to business. Managers spend 80 percent of their time in direct communication with others and the other 20 percent on desk work, much of which is also communication in the form of writing and reading. Communicators need to pay attention to audience feedback, even solicit it, to determine whether their message was perceived in the way they intended.

2.   The six elements involved in communication are: sender, message, channel, audience, feedback, and context.

Learning Goal 9.7
Listing
1.   Nonverbal communication
2.   Verbal communication
3.   Informal communication
4.   Oral communication
5.   Written communication
6.   Formal communication

Multiple Choice
7. d   8. d   9. b   10. b

Learning Goal 9.8
The ability to communicate cross-culturally is becoming more and more important in business due to the globalization of business. Communication in low-context cultures tends to rely of explicit written and verbal messages. In high-context cultures, however, it is more likely to depend not only on the message itself, but also on everything that surrounds it, such as nonverbal cues and the personal relationship between the communicators. American businesspeople must temper their low-context style when in high-context cultures.

Learning Goal 9.9
Various communication technologies---computers, videoconferencing, electronic mail, networks---can influence the efficiency of communication by making it easier to create, organize, and distribute messages. They also facilitate international transactions by minimizing time differences and making all areas of the world more accessible.

Self-Review
True or False
1. F	4. T	7. T	10. F	13. F
2. T	5. F	8. T	11. F	14. T
3. T	6. F	9. T	12. T	

Multiple Choice
1. a	4. e	7. d	10. d
2. e	5. a	8. e	
3. b	6. a	9. b	

Application Exercises

1.
- a. The "avoiding style" would likely be most appropriate in this case because the cause of the conflict is trivial.
- b. The "competing style" would likely be most appropriate in this case because this is an unpopular decision.
- c. The "compromising style" would likely be most appropriate in this case because two opposing goals are equally important.
- d. The "accommodating style" would likely be most appropriate in this case because the work-aholic would be expected to back down because having Saturdays off for families and leisure activity is more important to others in the group. Moreover, there is no need for rushing at this point.
- e. The "collaborating style" would likely be most appropriate in this case because the viewpoints of all participants (workers and management) must be merged into a mutually acceptable solution. Consensus needs to be achieved to arrive at a win-win situation.

2. A team leader can reduce conflict by focusing team members of broad goals, clarifying participants' respective tasks and areas of authority, acting as a mediator, and facilitating effective communication.

3. It is extremely important for a manager to be a good listener---an active listener. In order for appropriate decisions to be made by management then information is important. Active listening is necessary if the message is to be properly received. Indeed, active listening is the basis for effective communication. Moreover, effective managers often find that by listening to employees----acting as a sound board---employees will discover the answers to their concerns themselves. Or, the manager can lead the discussion toward the employee "discovering" the "answer" themselves. In this way, employees help arrive at the solution to the problem, are more apt to see to it that the "solution" is realized, and their self-esteem is enhanced in the process (increasing their motivation; making them feel that their input is important, as it should be). Good active listening skills on the part

190

of management is absolutely essential to enhance productivity and profitability of a company.

4.   A cross-functional team involves employees from different departments who work together on specific projects, such as developing a new product or solving a particular problem. A cross-functional team has the advantage of pooling talent from diverse areas within the organization increasing the range of viewpoints. In the process, the bigger picture can be more clearly seen by all members of the team. For example, what may make since from an engineering perspective may not always make sense from a marketing perspective, etc...

     Cross-functional teams created to develop a new product will likely result in a better product, all things considered, being introduced in the market. If the team was designed to solve a particular problem, then it is more likely the proposal put forth by the cross-functional team will be the all-around most appropriate. Moreover, the input and cooperation between the different departments represented on the team will likely increase the chances that all departments will work together (as opposed to competing) to realize the agreed upon goal.

Crossword Puzzle

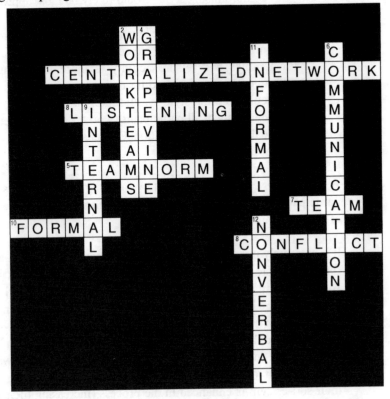

CHAPTER 9

Chapter 10

Information for Decision Making

"Someone once gave the recipe for effective decisions as '90 percent information and 10 percent inspiration.' Clearly, obtaining the right information and knowing how to use it are vital to business success." (212)

KEY CONCEPTS

Management information system (MIS)	An organized method for providing past, present, and projected information on internal operations and external intelligence for use in decision making. (213)
Chief information officer (CIO)	An executive responsible for directing the firm's MIS and related computer operations. (213)
Database	A centralized, integrated collection of the organization's data resources. (213)
Computer	A programmable electronics device that can store, retrieve, and process data. (213)
Hardware	All the tangible elements of the computer system. (214)
Software	Sets of instructions that tell the hardware what to do. (214)
Microcomputer	The smallest type of computer. (214)
Telecommunications	Any system in which information or data are sent over a distance through some type of transmission medium. (216)
Information superhighways	Merging telecommunications, information, and data networks into a single, enormous pathway accessible to all consumers and businesses. (216)
Computer networks	Systems that interconnect numerous computers so they function individually or communicate with each other. (217)

192

Local area network (LAN)	A computer network that connects machines within a limited area. (218)
Word processing	The use of computers to type, store, retrieve, edit, and print various types of documents. (219)
Desktop publishing	A computer system that allows companies to design and produce printed material in-house. (219)
Decision support system (DSS)	A system that quickly provides relevant facts to help business people make decisions. (220)
Spreadsheet	The computerized equivalent of an accountant's worksheet. (220)
Electronic mail (E-mail)	A system for sending and receiving written messages from one computer to another via phone lines. (221)
Expert systems	Computer programs that imitate human thinking through a complicated series of "if... then" rules. (222)
Multimedia computing	The technologies that facilitate the integration of two or more types of media. (223)
Interactive media	Program applications that allow users to interact with computers to perform different functions at the same time. (223)
Groupware	Computer software that combines and extends the concept of shared information (a database) with a method for moving data between users (E-mail). (224)

Name:_____**Professor:**_____

Section:_____**Date:**_____

ANALYSIS OF LEARNING GOALS

Learning Goal 10.1

Explain the purpose of an information system and how it aids decision making in business.
(212-213)

True or False

__F__1.   A management information system is an organized method for providing past, present, and projected information on internal operations but provides little information about external information on consumers.

__F__2.   A chief information officer is the same as the chief executive officer.

__T__3.   Management information systems should aid in virtually all areas of the organization

__T__4.   Progressive companies use management information systems every day in making business decisions.

__T__5.   A data base is a centralized, integrated collection of the organization's data resources.

Learning Goal 10.2

List the major contributions and limitations of computers. (213-214)

Describe

Describe the major advantages and disadvantages associated with the use of computers in business.

194

Learning Goal 10.3
Distinguish among mainframe computers, minicomputers, and microcomputers. (215)

Fill in the blank

The primary basis for distinction among the three types of computers is _____.

The largest computer is called a *Mainframe*_____. It has the largest storage capacity and

the fastest processing speed. *Minicomputer* are smaller (about the size of filing

cabinets), less powerful, and less expensive. *Microcomputers*, the smallest type of

computers, include desktops, notepads, and pocket computers that have limited storage systems

but are portable. Each type of computer contains the basic elements of any computer system.

Learning Goal 10.4
Distinguish between hardware and software. (214)

Describe

Describe the difference between hardware and software.

Learning Goal 10.5
Discuss the role of telecommunications in business. (216-219)

True or False

___T___ 1.   Telecommunications refers to any system in which information or data are sent over a distance through some type of transmission medium.

___T___ 2.   Telecommunications involves such technologies as computer networks, telephones, television, facsimile (fax) machines, and wireless communications.

___T___ 3.   Telecommunications and computer networks are useful because they can link microcomputers and allow them to share printers and information, even if they are not in the same location.

___F___ 4.   A computer network is all of the tangible elements of a computer system.

Learning Goal 10.6
Explain the concept of an information superhighway and its implications for business.
(216; 226-227)

---

1.   What is an information superhighway?

2.   What are the advantages of an information superhighway?

196

Learning Goal 10.7

Describe the major business applications of computers. (219-224)

Matching

Match the following terms with the statements below.

a.   word processing
b.   desktop publishing
c.   decision support system DSS)
d.   spreadsheet
e.   Electronic mail (E-mail)
f.   Executive information system (EIS)

g.   Expert systems
h.   Voice processing
i.   Multimedia computing
j.   interactive media
k.   groupware

_C_ 1.   A system that quickly provides relevant facts to help business people make decisions.

_A_ 2.   The use of computers to type, store, retrieve, edit, and print various types of documents.

_K_ 3.   Computer software that combines and extends the concept of shared information (a database) with a method for moving data between users (E-mail).

_G_ 4.   Computer programs that imitate human thinking through a complicated series of "if... then" rules.

_J_ 5.   Program applications that allow users to interact with computers to perform different functions at the same time.

_B_ 6.   A computer system that allows companies to design and produce printed material in-house.

_E_ 7.   A system for sending and receiving written messages from one computer to another via phone lines.

_I_ 8.   The technologies that facilitate the integration of two or more types of media.

_D_ 9.   The computerized equivalent of an accountant's worksheet.

F   10.   Allows top managers to access the firm's primary databases.

H   11.   Involves technologies that use spoken language to send or receive information
           from a computer.

Learning Goal 10.8
Summarize the major computer security issues that affect organizations. (224-226)

Describe

Summarize the major computer security issues that affect organizations.

Name:_____ **Professor:**_____

Section:_____ **Date:**_____

SELF REVIEW

True or False

T   1.   Effective decisions cannot be made without answers to questions about the internal operations of the firm and the external environment in which it operates.

F   2.   Data bases can only be used by firms who collect and store their own information.

F   3.   There are really no disadvantages associated with businesses using computers.

F   4.   Minicomputers are the smallest type of computers, which include desktops.

T   5.   A microcomputer, typically called a personal computer or PC, has a video display terminal (VDT) that displays output on a TV-like screen.

F   6.   Computer software consists of all the tangible elements of the computer system; whereas hardware consists of computer languages and special programs that tell the computer what to do.

T   7.   Computer networks make it easier for people to obtain and share information, even if they are not in the same location.

T   8.   A local area network (LAN) is a computer network that connects machines within a limited area.

F   9.   The information superhighway will, in practice, unfortunately increase the time necessary to transmit information and will reduce the pace of work.

T   10.   A spreadsheet presents a grid of columns and rows that allows information to be organized in a standardized, easily understandable format.

T   11.   Speech recognition systems that allow computers to "understand" and respond to the human voice are still more common in science fiction than in business.

T   12.   Expert systems apply human knowledge to problems in specific subject areas in order to solve problems.

T   13.   A computer virus is a program that secretly attaches itself to other programs and changes them or destroys the data kept on a disk.

200

Multiple Choice

1. Management information systems:
    a. provides past and present information on internal operations and external intelligence for use in decision making, but presently is unable to make projections about the future.
    b. are helpful for only the largest companies.
    c. is useful in only certain areas of a business organization.
    d. is often the responsibility of an executive called the chief information officer (CIO).
    e. is the direct responsibility of the chief executive officer (CEO).

2. A data base:
    a. is a centralized, integrated collection of the organization's data resources.
    b. can be thought of as an electronic filing cabinet, capable of storing massive amounts of data and retrieving needed data within seconds.
    c. is available to firms who cannot afford to create and maintain their own by subscribing to commercial database services providing by companies who specialize in doing just this sort of thing.
    d. can be very helpful in finding out more about prospective customers.
    e. all of the above

3. Which of the following is *not* an disadvantage associated with the use of computers in business?
    a. Computers make volumes of data available quickly.
    b. Computers can be very expensive.
    c. Computers can be relied on too heavily.
    d. Computers can alienate customers.
    e. Computers can make mistakes if improperly programmed.

4. Which of the following statement is true about the different types of computers?
    a. A mainframe computer is the least expensive type of computer.
    b. The minicomputer is the smallest type of computer.
    c. The desktop and notepad computers are examples of microcomputers.
    d. The primary basis for distinction among the three types of computers is the basic elements found in the computer system.
    e. The microcomputer possesses the greatest storage capacity and the fastest processing speed.

5.   The personal computer (PC) is:
    a.   a mainframe computer.
    b.   a minicomputer.
    c.   a microcomputer.
    d.   rarely used in business.
    e.   used less today in business than in the past.

6.   Which of the following is *not* considered to be part of the hardware features of a computer system?
    a.   All of the tangible elements of the computer system.
    b.   The computer language and special programs that tell the computer what to do.
    c.   The input devices that store and process data and perform required calculations.
    d.   The output devices that communicate the results to the computer user.
    e.   The computer chip.

7.   Which of the following statements is true concerning the role of telecommunications in business?
    a.   Telecommunications refers to any system in which information or data are sent over a distance through some type of transmission medium.
    b.   Telecommunications involves such technologies as computer networks, telephones, television, facsimile (fax) machines, and wireless communications.
    c.   Telecommunications and computer networks are useful because they can link microcomputers and allow them to share printers and information, even if they are not in the same location.
    d.   A computer network is a system that interconnects numerous computers so they function individually or communicate with each other.
    e.   All of the above.

8.   The information superhighway will:
    a.   play a greater role in business as more and more applications are developed.
    b.   will reduce the access households have to information.
    c.   create a barrier for doing business internationally.
    d.   have little impact on business relationships.
    e.   do all of the above.

9. Desktop publishing is:
   - a. a computer system that allows companies to design and produce printed material in-house.
   - b. a system that quickly provides relevant facts to help business people make decisions.
   - c. the computerized equivalent of an accountant's worksheet.
   - d. a program application that allows users to interact with computers to perform different functions at the same time.
   - e. the use of technologies that facilitate the integration of two or more types of media.

10. A decision support system (DSS) is:
    - a. the use of computers to type, store, retrieve, edit, and print various types of documents.
    - b. a system that quickly provides relevant facts to help business people make decisions.
    - c. a computer program that imitates human thinking through a complicated series of "if... then" rules.
    - d. a system for sending and receiving written messages from one computer to another via phone lines.
    - e. a computer software that combines and extends the concept of shared information (a database) with a method for moving data between users (E-mail).

11. Interactive media is:
    - a. a computer programs that imitate human thinking through a complicated series of "if... then" rules.
    - b. a computer software that combines and extends the concept of shared information (a database) with a method for moving data between users (E-mail).
    - c. the technologies that facilitate the integration of two or more types of media.
    - d. program applications that allow users to interact with computers to perform different functions at the same time.
    - e. uses computers to type, store, retrieve, edit, and print various types of documents.

12. Which of the following statement is true?
    - a. Networks reduce the security problems associated with using computers.
    - b. Power failures no longer pose a threat to businesses reliant on computer usage.
    - c. Organizations need not go to the expense of a backup plan in the event of a computer failure because the probability of a computer failure is so low.
    - d. When computers are connected to a network, a problem at any location can affect the entire network.
    - e. Computer crime is not a substantial problem in the United States.

Name:_____Professor:_____
Section:_____Date:_____

APPLICATION EXERCISES

1.   Who stands to gain from an information superhighway? Who might lose?

2.   Should a company necessarily purchase the latest MIS technology? Why, or why not?

204

3.   How can a business try to overcome the disadvantages associated with the use of computers?

4.   What are some recommendations for protecting against computer viruses?

Name:_____**Professor:**_____
Section:_____**Date:**_____

ACROSS

1. Systems that interconnect numerous computers so they function individually or communicate with each other. (2 words)

3. All the tangible elements of the computer system.

7. A programmable electronics device that can store, retrieve, and process data.

DOWN

2. Sets of instructions that tell the hardware what to do.

4. A centralized, integrated collection of the organization's data resources.

5. The computerized equivalent of an accountant's worksheet.

6. Computer programs that imitate human thinking through a complicated series of "if . . . then" rules. (2 words)

8. Computer software that combines and extends the concept of shared information (a database) with a method for moving data between users (E-mail).

9. The smallest type of computer.

10. The type of computing in which there are technologies that facilitate the integration of two or more types of media.

CHAPTER 10 SOLUTIONS

Analysis of Learning Goals

Learning Goal 10.1
1. False
2. False
3. True
4. True
5. True

Learning Goal 10.2
The advantages of using computers in business include:
    1.   They can store large amounts of information in a small amount of space and quickly make this information available for decision makers.
    2.   By performing the mechanical, routine, boring work of recording and maintaining incoming information, they can free people for more challenging work.

The disadvantages of using computers in business include:
    1.   They can be expensive.
    2.   They can make disastrous mistakes when programmed incorrectly.
    3.   They can become a crutch rather than a tool in decision making when they are relied on too heavily.
    4.   They can alienate customers.

Learning Goal 10.3
Size
Mainframe
Minicomputers
Microcomputers

Learning Goal 10.4
    Computer hardware consists of all the tangible elements of the computer system. These include input devices, the machines that store and process data and perform required calculations, and output devices that communicate the results to the computer user.
    Software consists of computer languages and special programs that tell the computer what to do.

Learning Goal 10.5
1. True   2. True   3. True   4. False

208

Learning Goal 10.6

1. An information superhighway is the merging of telecommunications, information, and data networks into a single, enormous pathway accessible to all consumers and businesses.

2. One advantage of an information superhighway is that it will give businesses and residences access to libraries, databases, teleconferencing, and many other services. Another advantage is that it will reduce the time necessary to transmit data and will speed up the pace of work. Also, it will overcome geographic barriers, and restructure business relationships by reducing the need for intermediaries.

Learning Goal 10.7

1. c
2. a
3. k
4. g
5. j
6. b
7. e
8. i
9. d
10. f
11. h

Learning Goal 10.8

Important computer security issues include natural disasters, power failures, equipment malfunctions, human error, computer crime, and computer viruses. When computers are connected to a network, a problem at any location can affect the entire network. Organizations need to be prepared with backup plans so they can continue operating if their computer system fails.

Self-Review

True or False

1. T	4. F	7. T	10. T	13. T
2. F	5. T	8. T	11. T	
3. F	6. F	9. F	12. T	

Multiple Choice

1. d	4. c	7. e	10. b
2. e	5. c	8. a	11. d
3. a	6. b	9. a	12. d

Application Exercises

1. Those businesses who stand to gain from an information superhighway are those who supply the services (software, etc.) that will be demanded. Also, those businesses who have access to the superhighway---those who are linked to the network----will benefit by being more accessible to customers. Those businesses who are not linked into the network will lose out on business---consumers may not have access to these businesses. That is why it is imperative that businesses of all sizes establish at least some expertise in management information systems and the use of computers in general. This may require businesses to spend some money and energy in training workers to use computers or to upgrade their skills.

    Likewise, consumers who have access to the information superhighway stand to gain while those who do not have access to computers or who do not know how to use computers will likely be left behind.

2. No. A firm should purchase computer hardware and software only if the benefits outweigh the costs. The benefits to a company of purchasing the latest technology may not justify the costs. A business should shop around and find the system which is best for *its* needs.

3. A business can try to be economical with the purchases of computer hardware and software. It can train its workers to more effectively take advantage of hardware and software to avoid costly mistakes associated with their use. A business should also recognize the limitations associated with the use of computers. Business people need to resist being mesmerized by fancy equipment and quantitative computer solutions to decision making. Businesses should also remember there are limits to the use of computers if the human touch is an integral part of their business, which is especially true in service sector industries where the human element often plays a major role in satisfying consumers' needs. Finally, businesses need to address computer security issues.

4. See the list on page 226 of the textbook.

210

Crossword Puzzle

CHAPTER 10

Marketing Management
and Customer Satisfaction

"Marketing is the link between the organization and the consumer." (234)

KEY CONCEPTS

Marketing	The process of planning and executing the conception, pricing, promotion, and distribution of ideas, goods, and services to create exchanges that satisfy individual and organizational objectives. (234)
Exchange	The process by which two or more parties trade things of value, so that each party feels it is better off after the trade. (235)
Marketing concept	Adopting a consumer orientation in order to achieve long-term success. (236)
Added value	When a good or service attains increased worth by delivering more than expected---something of personal significance to the customer. (236)
Customer satisfaction measurement (CSM) program	A procedure for measuring customer feedback against customer satisfaction goals and developing an action plan for improvement. (237)
Person marketing	Refers to a program designed to enhance the favorable opinion of an individual by selected others. (239)
Place marketing	Refers to attempts to attract people to a particular area, such as a city, state, or nation. (239)
Cause marketing	Refers to the marketing of a social cause or issue. (239)
Event marketing	The marketing of sporting, cultural, and charitable activities to selected target markets. (239)

212

Organization marketing	Attempts to influence others to accept the goals of, receive the services of, or contribute in some way to an organization. (239)
Market	Consists of people with purchasing power and the authority to buy. (239)
Consumer products	Those goods and services purchased by the ultimate consumer for his or her own use. (240)
Business products	Sometimes called organizational or industrial products---are goods and services purchased to be used, either directly or indirectly, in the production of other goods for resale. (240)
Target market	The group of consumers toward whom a firm will direct its marketing efforts. (240)
Marketing mix	A combination of the firm's product, pricing, distribution, and promotion strategies. (240)
Relationship marketing	An organization's attempt to develop long-term, cost-effective links with individual customers for mutual benefit. (241)
Consumer behavior	Consists of actions that are involved directly in obtaining, consuming, and disposing of products, including the decision processes that precede and follow these actions. (244)
Marketing research	The information function that ties the marketer to the marketplace. (245)
Market segmentation	The process of dividing the total market into several relatively homogeneous groups. (247)

Name:_____ Professor:_____
Section:_____ Date:_____

ANALYSIS OF LEARNING GOALS

Learning Goal 11.1
Discuss how marketing's role in the exchange process creates utility. (234-235)

True or False

T 1. Marketing is the process of planning and executing the conception, pricing, promotion, and distribution of ideas, foods, and services to create exchanges that satisfy individual and organizational objectives.

T 2. Exchange is the process by which two or more parties trade things of value, so that each party feels it is better off after the trade.

T 3. Marketing creates utility---the want satisfying power of a good or service---by having the product available when and where the consumer wants to buy it and by arranging for an orderly transfer of ownership.

F 4. While marketing creates form utility, production creates time, place, and ownership utility.

Listing

List the type of utility described by each of the following statements.

Ownership Utility 5. Arranging for an orderly transfer of ownership.

Form Utility 6. Converting raw materials into finished goods and services.

Place Utility 7. Utility created by having the good or service in the right place when the consumer wants to purchase it.

Time Utility 8. Utility created by having the good or service available when the consumer wants to purchase it.

Learning Goal 11.2
List the major functions of marketing. (236)

Matching

Match the following eight functions of marketing with the statements below.

a.   Buying   e.   Standardization and grading
b.   Selling   f.   Financing
c.   Transporting   g.   Risk taking
d.   Storing   h.   Providing marketing information

_a,b_ 1.   These two functions of marketing are the exchange functions of marketing.

_d_ 2.   The warehousing of goods until they are needed.

_g_ 3.   Taking into account uncertainties about future consumer behavior.

_c_ 4.   The physical movement of the product from the seller to the buyer.

_f_ 5.   Extending credit to consumers, wholesalers, and retailers.

_e_ 6.   Deals with standardizing the description of goods.

_h_ 7.   Determining what will sell and who will buy it.

Learning Goal 11.3
Explain the importance of the marketing concept and customer satisfaction in achieving success in the marketplace. (236-237)

True or False

_F_ 1.   The marketing concept can be defined as the ability of a good or service to meet or exceed buyer needs and expectations.

_F_ 2.   Consumer satisfaction can be defined as adopting a consumer orientation in order to achieve long-term success.

___T___3.   Consumer satisfaction is the true measure of quality.

___T___4.   A good or service with added value attains increased worth by delivering more
than expected---something of personal significance to the customer.

Learning Goal 11.4
*Outline methods for obtaining customer feedback and
measuring customer satisfaction.*(237-239)

---

1.   How can companies obtain feedback from their customers?

2.   How might a company measure customer satisfaction?

216

Learning Goal 11.5
Outline how a marketing strategy is developed. (239)

Listing
List the five types of not-for-profit marketing as described by the following statements.

Person marketing 1. Refers to a program designed to enhance the favorable opinion of an individual by selected others.

Cause 2. Refers to the marketing of a social cause or issue.

Organization 3. Attempts to influence others to accept the goals of, receive the services of, or contribute in some way to an organization.

Place 4. Refers to attempts to attract people to a particular area, such as a city, state, or nation.

Event 5. The marketing of sporting, cultural, and charitable activities to selected target markets.

Describe
6. What are the three elements of a marketing strategy?

7. What is a marketing plan?

Learning Goal 11.6
Explain the concept of a market. (239-241)

Fill in the Blank

A _market_ consists of people with purchasing power and the authority to buy.

Markets can be classified on the basis of the types of products they handle.

Consumer products are those goods and services purchased by the ultimate

consumer for his or her own use. _Business_ products (also known as industrial or

organizational goods) are products purchased to be used, directly or indirectly, in the production

of other products for resale. Having analyzed the market, the next step is to select a

target market---the group of consumers toward whom a firm will direct its

marketing efforts. The final step is creating a _marketing mix_ to satisfy the needs of the

target market. This is a combination of the firm's product, pricing, distribution, and promotion

strategies.

Learning Goal 11.7
Discuss why the study of consumer behavior is important to marketing. (244)

True or False

___T___ 1.   By studying consumer behavior marketing can identify consumers' attitudes toward their products and how they use them.

___T___ 2.   Both personal and interpersonal factors influence consumer behavior.

___F___ 3.   Personal influences on consumer behavior include cultural, social, and family influences.

___F___ 4.   Interpersonal determinants of consumer behavior include people's needs and motives, perceptions, attitudes, learned experiences, and self concepts.

218

---

1.   What is marketing research? What information does it provide?

2.   List the five basic reasons marketers conduct research?

3.   What else do marketers do beyond collecting information?

Learning Goal 11.9
List and explain the bases used to segment markets. (247-248)

Listing

List the methods of market segmentation used by marketers in segmenting consumer markets as described by the following statements.

Demographic 1. Market segmentation on the bases of age, sex, and family life-cycle stage.

Geographic 2. Market segmentation on the bases of where someone lives.

Psychographic 3. Market segmentation on the bases of behavioral and lifestyle profiles.

Product-related 4. Market segmentation on the bases of such things as the benefits that consumers seek when buying a product, or the degree of brand loyalty they feel toward it.

Describe

Describe the methods of market segmentation used by marketers in segmenting business markets?

Learning Goal 11.10
Explain the concept of relationship marketing. (241-242)

Describe
Describe what is meant by relationship marketing. Why is it an important trend in marketing?

Learning Goal 11.11
Identify the major components of the marketing environment. (242-244)

Matching
Match the following components of the marketing environment with the statements below.

a. Competitive
b. Political and legal
c. Economic

d. Technological
e. Social and cultural environment

_____A_____ 1. Changes in the marketing activities of competitors.

_____d_____ 2. Changes in "know-how" have a significant impact on how marketers design, produce, price , distribute, and promote their goods and services.

_____b_____ 3. Laws designed to maintain a competitive environment and to protect customers.

_____e_____ 4. Differences in people's values, customs, or language.

_____c_____ 5. Factors such as inflation, unemployment, and business cycles influence how much consumers spend and what they buy.

Name:_____ **Professor:**_____
Section:_____ **Date:**_____
SELF REVIEW
True or False

___T___ 1.   While production creates form utility, marketing creates time, place, and ownership utility.

___T___ 2.   Marketing creates utility by having the product available when and where the consumer wants to buy it and by arranging for an orderly transfer of ownership.

___F___ 3.   The risk taking function of marketing involves the warehousing of goods until they are sold.

___T___ 4.   Customer satisfaction directly effects a company's profitability.

___T___ 5.   Any method which makes it easier for customers to complain is to a firm's advantage.

___T___ 6.   A marketing plan is a written document that expresses the firm's marketing strategy.

___F___ 7.   Person marketing refers to the marketing of a social cause or issue.

___T___ 8.   The marketing mix is the mechanism that allows the firm to match consumer needs with product offerings.

___F___ 9.   The target market is the combination of the firm's product, pricing, distribution, and promotion strategies.

___T___ 10.   The study of consumer behavior includes both consumer and business purchases.

___F___ 11.   Marketing research is the information function that links the consumer to the product.

___F___ 12.   Relationship marketing is the process of dividing the total market into several relatively homogeneous groups.

___F___ 13.   Methods of segmenting business markets include criteria based on demographic, geographic, psychographic, and product-related concerns.

___T___ 14.   Relationship marketing enables a firm to target their best customers.

222

Multiple Choice

1. The function of marketing which is designed to have the good or service available when the consumer wants to buy it creates:
    a. distribution utility.
    b. form utility.
    c. time utility
    d. place utility
    e. ownership utility.

2. Which of the following statements is true?
    a. Exchange is the process of planning and executing the conception, pricing, promotion, and distribution of ideas, foods, and services to create exchanges that satisfy individual and organizational objectives.
    b. Marketing is the process by which two or more parties trade things of value, so that each party feels it is better off after the trade.
    c. In addition to selling goods and services, marketing is also used to advocate ideas or viewpoints, and to educate people.
    d. Marketing creates form utility.
    e. Specialization and division of labor leads to reduced production and lower standards of living.

3. Which of the following statements is true about the functions of marketing?
    a. The risk taking function involves extending credit to consumers, wholesalers, and retailers.
    b. The financing function involves the warehousing of goods until they are needed.
    c. The storing function involves determining what will sell and who will buy it.
    d. The transporting function involves the physical movement of the product from the seller to the buyer.
    e. The standardization and grading function of marketing involves the buying and selling of the good or service.

4. Customer satisfaction:
    a. is the true measure of quality.
    b. can be defined as the ability of a good or service to meet or exceed buyer needs and expectations.
    c. is crucial to an organization's continued existence.
    d. may require added value.
    e. all of the above.

5.   Which of the following is *not* part of a typical customer satisfaction measurement (CSM) program?
      a.   Providing a money-back guarantee.
      b.   Determine what areas are most critical to the business and what measurement systems currently are being used.
      c.   Probe a representative group of customers to learn what factors, or attributes, are important to their use of a good or service.
      d.   Conduct research to determine the company's performance on the selected attributes.
      e.   Analyze results to develop action plans.

6.   The marketing of sporting, cultural, and charitable activities to selected target markets is known as :
      a.   Person marketing.
      b.   Event marketing.
      c.   Organizational marketing.
      d.   Cause marketing.
      e.   Place marketing.

7.   A marketing plan includes:
      a.   a target market.
      b.   sales and revenue goals.
      c.   a marketing budget.
      d.   an indication of the timing of the marketing mix elements
      e.   all of the above.

8.   The marketing mix is a combination of the firm's:
      a.   product, pricing, distribution, and promotion strategies.
      b.   styling, engineering, pricing and guarantee strategies.
      c.   advertising, warehousing, production and scheduling strategies.
      d.   profit, location, type of good or service produced, and target market strategies.
      e.   employees, management, product, and pricing strategies.

9.   The study of consumer behavior:
      a.   is interested in why consumers buy the products they do; not how consumers use these items.
      b.   helps marketers develop more effective marketing strategies for reaching their customers.
      c.   is interested in personal but not cultural factors influencing consumer behavior.
      d.   includes the study of consumer but not business purchases.
      e.   all of the above.

224

10.   Which of the following is *not* one of the reasons marketers conduct marketing research?
      a.   To provide jobs in the marketing department.
      b.   To analyze competitor's strategies.
      c.   To evaluate and predict consumer behavior.
      d.   To identify marketing problems and opportunities.
      e.   To develop price, promotion, and distribution plans.

11.   Marketing research:
      a.   provides the information about potential target markets that is necessary to design effective marketing strategies.
      b.   is concerned with both internal and external data.
      c.   often involves government publications as sources of data.
      d.   is valuable only when it can be used to make decisions within the framework of the organization's strategic plan.
      e.   all of the above.

12.   Market segmentation:
      a.   of consumer goods and services is based on demographic, geographic, psychographic and product-related criteria.
      b.   occurs with the marketing of consumer products but not business products.
      c.   occurs only in the United States.
      d.   on the basis of demographic criteria refers to dividing up markets on a map.
      e.   on the basis of geographic criteria refers to dividing up markets according to different behavioral and lifestyle profiles.

13.   Which of the following is part of the marketing environment?
      a.   Price.
      b.   Product.
      c.   Consumer protection laws.
      d.   Distribution.
      e.   Promotion.

14.   Which of the following statements is correct?
      a.   Relationship marketing refers to the social and cultural environment in which marketing takes place.
      b.   The "marketing environment" refers to the geographic location of a market.
      c.   Marketing a good or service overseas means the firm must choose between standardization---selling the same product to every market----and adaptation---modifying products to fit each market.
      d.   An advantage to adapting a good to a foreign market is usually lower costs.
      e.   Marketing standardized products abroad usually works best for consumer goods.

Name:_____**Professor:**_____
Section:_____**Date:**_____

APPLICATION EXERCISES

1. Product differentiation occurs when a firm distinguishes its good or service in either real or imaginary terms from its competitors. Product differentiation can be an effective way for a firm to create a niche in the market for itself, or to gain market share. What are some examples of real and imaginary product differentiation? How is product differentiation related to the marketing mix?

2. How are product differentiation, the target market and market research related?

226

3.   How is the "appropriate" marketing mix and market segmentation related?

4.   Price discrimination is charging different people different prices for the same good or service where these price differences are not a result of cost differences. Price discrimination is undertaken by firms in order to increase profits. Market segmentation is the process of dividing the total market into several relatively homogeneous groups. How can price discrimination and market segmentation be related?

Name:_____ Professor:_____
Section:_____ Date:_____

CROSSWORD PUZZLE

ACROSS

1. Consists of actions that are involved directly in obtaining, consuming, and disposing of products, including the decision processes that precede and follow these actions. (2 words)

4. The process of planning and executing the conception, pricing, promotion, and distribution of ideas, goods, and services to create exchanges that satisfy individual and organizational objectives.

5. The group of consumers toward whom a firm will direct its marketing efforts. (2 words)

7. The process by which two or more parties trade things of value, so that each party feels it is better off after the trade.

9. Consists of people with purchasing power and the authority to buy.

DOWN

2. Those goods and services purchased by the ultimate consumer for his or her own use. (2 words)

3. The information function that ties the marketer to the market place. (2 words)

6. A good or service with this attains increased worth by delivering more than expected— something of personal significance to the customer. (2 words)

8. The marketing of sporting, cultural, and charitable activities to selected target markets. (2 words)

10. Refers to a program designed to enhance the favorable opinion of an individual by selected others. (2 words)

11. A combination of the firm's product, pricing, distribution and promotion strategies. (2 words)

CHAPTER 11 SOLUTIONS

Analysis of Learning Goals

Learning Goal 11.1
True or False
1. True
2. True
3. True
4. False

Matching
5. Ownership utility
6. Form utility
7. Place utility
8. Time utility

Learning Goal 11.2
1. *a* and *b*
2. d
3. g
4. c
5. f
6. e
7. h

Learning Goal 11.3
1. False   2. False   3. True   4. True

Learning Goal 11.4
1.   Companies can obtain feedback from their customers in a number of ways. These include: monitoring complaints; monitoring feedback from warranties and from toll-free phone service lines; visiting clients; calling them; sending out written surveys; or hiring "mystery shoppers."

230

2. A company can measure customer satisfaction by initiating a customer satisfaction measurement (CSM) program. CSM programs involve:
   1. Determining what areas are most critical to the business and what measurement systems currently are being used.
   2. Probe a representative group of customers to learn what factors, or attributes, are important to their use of a good or service.
   3. Conduct research to determine the company's performance on the selected attributes.
   4. Analyze results to develop action plans.

Learning Goal 11.5
Listing
1. Person marketing
2. Cause marketing
3. Organization marketing
4. Place marketing
5. Event marketing

Describe
6. The three elements of a marketing strategy are:
   1. An analysis of the market.
   2. Selecting a target market.
   3. Developing a marketing mix.

7. A marketing plan is a written document that expresses the firm's marketing strategy. Target market, sales and revenue goals, marketing budget, and timing of the marketing mix elements are included in the marketing plan.

Learning Goal 11.6
Market
Consumer
Business
Target
Marketing mix

Learning Goal 11.7
1. True   2. True   3. False   4. False

Learning Goal 11.8
1.   Marketing research is the information function that links the marketer to the marketplace. It provides the information about potential target markets that is necessary to design effective marketing mixes.

2.   Marketers conduct research for the five following reasons.
    1.   To identify marketing problems and opportunities.
    2.   To analyze competitor's strategies.
    3.   To evaluate and predict consumer behavior.
    4.   To gauge the performance of existing products and package designs as well as assessing the potential of new ones.
    5.   To develop price, promotion, and distribution plans.

3.   Researchers must also decide how to collect the information, interpret the results, and communicate the results.

Learning Goal 11.9
Listing
1.   Demographic
2.   Geographic
3.   Psychographic
4.   Product-related

Describe
Business marketers segment markets according to three criteria: geographic characteristics; customer-based specifications for products; and end-use applications, or the precise way in which the business purchaser will use the product.

Learning Goal 11.10
Relationship marketing is an organization's attempt to develop long-term, cost-effective links with individual customers for mutual benefit. It is an important trend in marketing because good relationships with customers can be a vital strategic tool for a firm. By identifying current purchasers and maintaining a positive relationship with them, organizations can target their best customers more efficiently.

Learning Goal 11.11
1. a
2. d
3. b
4. e
5. c

232

Self-Review

True or False

1. T	4. T	7. F	10. T	13. F
2. T	5. T	8. T	11. F	14. T
3. F	6. T	9. F	12. F	

Multiple Choice

1. c	4. e	7. e	10. a	13. c
2. c	5. a	8. a	11. e	14. c
3. d	6. b	9. b	12. a	

Application Exercises

1.   Examples of product differentiation in *real* terms include: producing a truly higher quality product; "smarter" packaging; more convenient shopping locations, hours of operation, or delivery service; better service after the sale; longer warranties; better credit conditions (lower interest charges or longer payment periods); etc. Examples of *imaginary* differences include the association of the good or service with "sex-appeal," "class," "status," or just "being cool." It is creating an image associated with the good or the service. This may be accomplished by having a well-known celebrity endorsing the good or service.

   The marketing mix is the combination of the firm's product, pricing, distribution and promotion strategies. Product differentiation focuses on successfully distinguishing the firm's good or service from the competition so that a higher price may be charged. This can be accomplished through unique and/or effective distribution and promotional strategies.

2.   Often, in order to successfully differentiate a good or service from competitors, a firm must know for whom the differentiation should be tailored. What is the target market? This requires knowledge of who these people are in the target market and what they want or need. That requires market research.

3.   What is considered the "appropriate" marketing mix (the "appropriate" product, at the "appropriate" price, distributed in the "appropriate" way, and promoted the "appropriate" way) depends upon the target market---that segment of the market one is focusing on. This is especially true when it comes to international marketing.

4.   By segmenting your market into groups of people who are more and less price sensitive then you can charge a higher price to those who are less price sensitive. Examples of price discrimination are the different prices charged by doctors and dentists (based on whether you have or do not have health insurance coverage), movie theaters (the evening showing of the same film is more expensive), golf courses (its more expensive to golf on the weekend), restaurants (the evening menu is more "pricey" than the lunch menu for virtually the same meal), lawyers (how much trouble have you been in before?), and electric utilities (residential customers are charged higher rates than commercial customers).

Crossword Puzzle

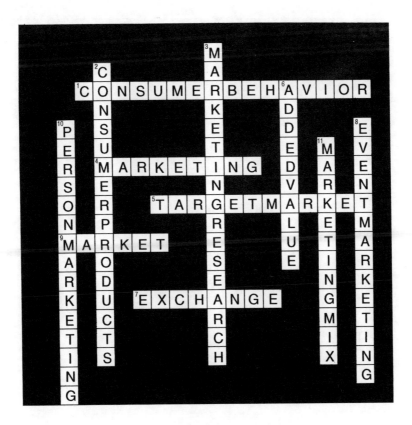

CHAPTER 11

Chapter 12

Creating and Producing World-Class Goods and Services

"The creation of new products is the lifeblood of an organization." (254)

KEY CONCEPTS

Brand	A name, term, sign, symbol, design, or some combination thereof used to identify the products of one firm and to differentiate them from competitive offerings. (255)
Brand name	That part of the brand consisting of words or letters included in a name used to identify and distinguish the firm's offerings from those of competitors. (255)
Trademark	A brand that has been given legal protection. (256)
National brand	A brand offered and promoted by a manufacturer. (257)
Private brand	A product that is not linked to the manufacturer, but instead carries a wholesaler's or the retailer's label. (Often known as a house, distributor, or retailer label.) (257)
Generic products	Products which have plain packaging, minimal labeling, little if any advertising, and meet only minimal quality standards. (258)
Family brand	A single brand name used for several related products. (258)
Individual branding	Giving products within a line different brand names. (258)
Production	The use of people and machinery to convert materials into finished foods and services. (258)
Production and operations management	To manage the use of people and machinery in converting materials and resources into finished goods and services. (258)

236

Mass production	The manufacture of products in large amounts through the effective combination of specialized labor, mechanization, and standardization. (259)
Assembly line	A manufacturing technique that involves placing the product on a conveyor belt that travels past a number of workstations where workers perform specialized tasks. (260)
Robot	A reprogammable machine capable of performing a variety of tasks requiring programmed manipulation of materials and tools. (262)
Computer-aided design (CAD)	Enables engineers to design parts and buildings on computer screens faster and with fewer mistakes than on paper. (263)
Computer-aided manufacturing (CAM)	Enables manufacturers to use special-design computers to analyze the necessary steps that a machine must perform to produce a needed product or part. (263)
Computer-integrated manufacturing (CIM)	The use of computers to design products, control machines, handle materials, and control the production function in an integrated fashion. (265)
Environmental impact study	Analyzes how the proposed plant would impact the quality of life in that area. (265)
Inventory control	Balances the need to have inventory on hand to meet demand with the costs involved in carrying inventory. (266)
JIT	Means "Just In Time." A broad management philosophy that reaches beyond the narrow activity of inventory control and influences the entire system of production and operations management. (267)
Quality control	Measuring goods and services against established quality standards. (268)

Name:_____**Professor:**_____

Section:_____**Date:**_____

ANALYSIS OF LEARNING GOALS

Learning Goal 12.1

Explain why product development is important to a firm. (254)

True or False

___T___ 1.   The firm's production function is responsible for creating *form* utility.

___T___ 2.   Products do not remain economically viable forever, so new ones must be developed to assure the survival of an organization.

___T___ 3.   For many firms, new products account for a sizable portion of sales and profits.

___T___ 4.   The creation of new products is the lifeblood of an organization.

Learning Goal 12.2

Lists the stages of new product development. (254-255)

Listing

Write out the correct order of the stages of new-product development.

a.   Screening   d.   Product development
b.   Business analysis   e.   Generate new product ideas
c.   Commercialization   f.   Test marketing

Generate new product ideas   1.   The first step in new-product development.

Screening   2.   The second step.

Business analysis   3.   The third step.

Product development   4.   The fourth step.

Test marketing   5.   This fifth step may be skipped by some firms out of fear it may reveal its product strategy to competitors.

Commercialization   6.   The final step in new-product development.

238

Learning Goal 12.3
Explain how products are identified. (255-258)

Fill in the Blank

Goods and services are identified by brands. brand names, and trademarks. A

Brand is a name, term, sign, symbol, design, or some combination thereof used

to identify the products of one firm and to differentiate them from competitive offerings. A

Brand name is that part of the brand consisting of works or letters included in a name

used to identify and distinguish the firm's offerings from those of competitors. A

trademark is a brand that has been given legal protection.

Matching

Match the following brand categories with their definitions.

a. national brand
b. private brand
c. generic products.

d. family brand
e. individual branding

A 1. A brand offered and promoted by a manufacturer.

C 2. Products which have plain packaging, minimal labeling, little if any advertising, and meet only minimal quality standards.

E 3. Giving products within a line different brand names.

B 4. A product that is not linked to the manufacturer, but instead carries a wholesaler's or the retailer's label. (Often known as a house, distributor, or retailer label.)

D 5. A single brand name used for several related products.

Learning Goal 12.4
Explain the strategic importance of production and operations management in an organization. (258-259)

Describe

Describe the strategic role of production and operations management.

Learning Goal 12.5
Compare mass production with newer production techniques. (259-262)

Describe

1.   What is mass production?

240

2.   What is a major advantages of mass production?

3.   What are some disadvantages of mass production?

Fill in the Blank

Fill in the following terms where appropriate.

Flexible production
Customer-driven production
Team concept

To become more competitive, many firms are adopting new approaches

to production. _Flexible production_ methods require fewer workers and less inventory, and

are cost-effective with smaller batches too. With _customer-driven production_ processes, customers'

demands determine what stores stock and, in turn, what manufacturers make. The

team concept combines employees from various departments and functions---such as

design, manufacturing, finance, and maintenance---to work together on designing and

building products.

Learning Goal 12.6
Discuss how computers and related technologies are revolutionizing product development and production. (262-265)

Describe

Discuss how computers and related technologies are revolutionizing product development and production.

Learning Goal 12.7
Outline the major factors involved in choosing plant locations. (265-266)

Listing

Factors involved in choosing the best location fall into three categories. List the factors described by each of the following statements.

Physical factors   1.   These factors involve such issues as water supply, available energy, and options for disposing of hazardous wastes.

Human factors   2.   These factors include the area's labor supply, local regulations, and living conditions.

Transportation factors   3.   These factors include proximity to markets and raw materials, and availability of transportation alternatives.

242

Learning Goal 12.8
Describe the major tasks of production and operations managers. (266)

Describe

Describe the major tasks of production and operations managers.

Learning Goal 12.9
Explain the importance of inventory control and just-in-time systems. (266-267)

True or False

T 1. Inventory control balances the need to have inventory on hand to meet demand with the costs involved in carrying inventory.

F 2. The higher costs of carrying more inventory usually accompany the greater probability of lost sales and unhappy customers.

T 3. Just-in-time (JIT) is a broad management philosophy that reaches beyond the narrow activity of inventory control and influences the entire system of production and operations management.

T 4. Just-in-time attempts to provide the right part at the right place at the right time.

Learning Goal 12.10
Discuss the benefits of quality control. (267-268)

---

1.   What is quality control?

2.   How does one ensure or check for quality control?

3.   How important is quality in product development?

Name:_____ Professor:_____
Section:_____ Date:_____

SELF REVIEW

True or False

T 1. The creation of new products is the lifeblood of an organization.

T 2. The commercialization stage of new-product development must be synchronized with the firm's promotional, distribution, and pricing strategies.

T 3. Generic words---words that describe a type of product---cannot be used exclusively by any organization.

F 4. A national brand identifies a product that is not linked to the manufacturer, but instead carries a wholesaler's or the retailer's label.

T 5. The task of production and operations management is to manage the use of people and machinery in converting materials and resources into finished goods and services.

F 6. Mass production usually raises per unit costs of production.

F 7. Mass production is usually profitable making small batches of products.

T 8. Automation allows companies to design and create new products faster, modify them more rapidly, and meet customers' changing needs more effectively.

T 9. A flexible manufacturing system (FMS) is a facility that can be modified quickly to manufacture different products.

F 10. The three most important factors involved the location decision of a firm are taxes, regulations, and how bad the community wants the firm.

F 11. The United States has the highest average labor costs in the world.

T 12. Just-in-time (JIT) inventory control shifts much of the responsibility for carrying inventory to suppliers operating on forecasts, since they are forced to keep more on hand to be responsive to manufacturers' needs.

T 13. If management concentrates on producing a quality product that satisfies the needs of its customers, a by product will be lower "costs of quality."

246

Multiple Choice

1. Which of the following stages in new product development may be skipped by a firm if it fears that this stage of development may reveal its product strategy?
    a. Screening.
    b. Generate new product ideas.
    c. Test marketing.
    d. Product development.
    e. Commercialization.

2. The screening stage of new-product development:
    a. is the starting point in new-product development.
    b. involves eliminating ideas if they do not mesh with overall company objectives or cannot be developed given the company's resources.
    c. is when the actual product is developed, subjected to a series of tests, and revised.
    d. involves the item being sold in a limited area while the company examines both the product and the marketing effort used to support it.
    e. occurs when the product is made generally available in the marketplace.

3. The stage of new-product development in which a firm assesses the new product's potential sales, profits, growth rate, and competitive strengths involves the:
    a. Screening stage
    b. the generation-of-new-product-ideas stage
    c. business analysis stage.
    d. product development stage.
    e. test marketing stage.

4. A private brand is:
    a. a brand offered and promoted by a manufacturer.
    b. a product which has plain packaging, minimal labeling, little if any advertising, and meets only minimal quality standards.
    c. when a product within a line has a different brand name.
    d. a product that is not linked to the manufacturer, but instead carries a wholesaler's or the retailer's label. (Often known as a house, distributor, or retailer label.)
    e. a single brand name used for several related products.

5. A brand that has been given legal protection is called a:
    a. national brand.
    b. private brand.
    c. generic brand.
    d. family brand.
    e. trademark.

---

6.   Production and operations management plays an important strategic role in business by:
      a.   lowering the costs of production.
      b.   boosting the quality of products.
      c.   and allowing the firm to respond flexibly and dependably to customers' demands.
      d.   all of the above.
      e.   none of the above.

7.   Mass production:
      a.   is the manufacture of products in large amounts through the effective combination of specialized labor, mechanization, and standardization.
      b.   usually results in lower per unit costs and therefore lower prices to consumers.
      c.   is less efficient for making small batches of different items.
      d.   can result in so much specialization that workers' jobs become boring.
      e.   all of the above.

8.   Which of the following statements is true concerning production systems?
      a.   Mass production rarely involves the use of an assembly line.
      b.   Flexible production methods require fewer workers and less inventory, and are cost-effective with smaller batches too.
      c.   Customer-driven production combines employees from various departments and functions---such as design manufacturing, finance, and maintenance---to work together on designing and building products.
      d.   With team concept production processes, customers' demands determine what stores stock and, in turn, what manufacturers make.
      e.   All of the above.

9.   Which of the following statements is true?
      a.   A robot is a reprogammable machine capable of performing a variety of tasks requiring programmed manipulation of materials and tools.
      b.   Computer-aided design (CAD) enables engineers to design parts and buildings on computer screens faster and with fewer mistakes than on paper.
      c.   Computer-aided manufacturing (CAM) enables manufacturers to use special-design computers to analyze the necessary steps that a machine must perform to produce a needed product or part.
      d.   Computer-integrated manufacturing (CIM) is the use of computers to design products, control machines, handle materials, and control the production function in an integrated fashion.
      e.   All of the above.

10.   Operations and production managers are responsible for:
   a.   planning the overall production process.
   b.   determining the best layout for the production facility.
   c.   implementing the production plan.
   d.   controlling the production process and evaluating results in order to maintain the highest possible quality.
   e.   all of the above.

11.   Which of the following statements is true about inventory control?
   a.   Inventory carrying costs are the costs associated with lost business when products or parts are not in stock.
   b.   The higher costs of carrying more inventory usually accompany the greater probability of lost sales and unhappy customers.
   c.   Just-in-time attempts to provide the right part at the right place at the right time.
   d.   Just-in-time has not been adopted by U.S. businesses.
   e.   Effective inventory control is a relatively unimportant matter for most manufacturing firms.

12.   The "costs of quality" refers to:
   a.   the production costs associated with inspecting items for quality.
   b.   those costs that result from not making the product right the first time.
   c.   the increased costs associated with selling more high quality products.
   d.   the higher prices consumers a re willing to pay to receive higher quality products.
   e.   the training costs associated with labor in order to produce a higher quality product.

Name:_____**Professor:**_____

Section:_____**Date:**_____

APPLICATION EXERCISES

1.   If you are a supplier of a component part to manufacturers, would you rather supply to a firm which uses just-in-time (JIT) inventory control or a firm which does not? Why?

2.   Most firms fail because of bad management. In particular, most firms fail because of cash-flow problems. How could mismanagement of inventory be related to cash-flow problems?

250

3.   How important is a quality labor force in a manufacturer's plant location decision? What kind of workers do you think most manufacturing firms are looking for in their location decision?   What's the relevance for public policy-makers interested in attracting manufacturing firms to their area in order to create jobs?

4.   How could producing a quality product and just-in-time (JIT) inventory control be complementary goals?

Name:_____ Professor:_____
Section:_____ Date:_____

CROSSWORD PUZZLE

ACROSS

1. Products which have plain packaging, minimal labeling, little if any advertising, and meet only minimal quality standards. (2 words)

3. That part of the brand consisting of words or letters included in a name used to identify and distinguish the firm's offerings from those of competitors. (2 words)

4. A product that is not linked to the manufacturer, but instead carries a wholesaler's or the retailer's label. (2 words)

5. A programmable machine capable of performing a variety of tasks requiring programmed manipulation of materials and tools.

6. A name, term, symbol, design, or some combination thereof used to identify the products of one firm and to differentiate them from competitive offerings.

DOWN

2. Balances the need to have inventory on hand to meet demand with the costs involved in carrying inventory. (2 words)

7. Giving products within a line different brand names. (2 words)

8. A brand that has been given legal protection.

9. A manufacturing technique that involves placing the product on a conveyor belt that travels past a number of workstations where workers perform specialized tasks. (2 words)

CHAPTER 12 SOLUTIONS

Analysis of Learning Goals

Learning Goal 12.1

1. True	2. True	3. True	4. True

Learning Goal 12.2

1. e. Generate new product ideas
2. a. Screening
3. b. Business analysis
4. d. Product development
5. f. Test marketing
6. c. Commercialization

Learning Goal 12.3

Fill in the Blank

Brand

Brand name

Trademark

Matching

1. a. national brand
2. c. generic products
3. e. individual branding
4. b. private brand
5. d. family brand

Learning Goal 12.4

Production and operations management plays an important strategic role by lowering the costs of production, boosting the quality of products, and allowing the firm to respond flexibly and dependably to customers' demands.

Learning Goal 12.5

Describe

1.   Mass production is the manufacture of products in large amounts through the effective combination of specialized labor, mechanization, and standardization.

2.   A major advantage of mass production is being able to produce large quantities of products cheaper and therefore making them available to consumers at lower prices than would have been possible had these products been crafted individually.

254

3.   Although mass production is highly efficient for making large quantities of similar products, it is less efficient for making small batches of different items. Furthermore, specialization can make worker's jobs boring.

Fill in the Blank
Flexible production
Customer-driven production
Team concept

Learning Goal 12.6
Automation allows companies to design and create new products faster, modify them more rapidly, and meet customers' changing needs more effectively. Important design and/or production technologies include robots, computer-aided design (CAD), computer-aided manufacturing (CAM), flexible manufacturing systems (FMS), and computer-integrated manufacturing (CIM).

Learning Goal 12.7
1. Physical factors
2. Human factors
3. Transportation factors

Learning Goal 12.8
Production and operations managers are responsible for overseeing the use of people and machinery to convert inputs into finished goods and services. This involves four major tasks. First, they must plan the overall production process. Second, they must determine the best layout for the production facility. Third, they must implement the production plan. Finally, they are responsible for controlling the production process and evaluating results in order to maintain the highest possible quality.

Learning Goal 12.9
1. True   2. False   3. True   4. True

Learning Goal 12.10
1.   Quality control is measuring goods and services against established quality standards.

2.   Quality control can be ensured by checking the items being produced. Such checks are necessary to spot defective products and to see that they are not shipped to customers. Devices for monitoring quality levels include visual inspection, electronic sensors, robots, and X-rays.

3.   Quality is vital in product development; investing more money up front in quality design

and development ultimately decreases the "costs of quality" (the costs that result from not producing the product right the first time).

Self-Review

True or False

1. T	4. F	7. F	10. F	13. T
2. T	5. T	8. T	11. F	
3. T	6. F	9. T	12. T	

Multiple Choice

1. c	4. d	7. e	10. e
2. b	5. e	8. b	11. c
3. c	6. d	9. e	12. b

Application Exercises

1.   If everything else is the same, you would prefer to sell to the manufacturer which does *not* use just-in-time (JIT). This is because firms which use JIT shift much of the responsibility for carrying inventory to suppliers, since they are forced to keep more on hand to be responsive to manufacturers' needs. Suppliers who cannot keep enough high-quality parts on hand often get dropped in favor of suppliers who can. Therefore, inventory carrying costs are higher to you if you supply to a manufacturer who uses JIT.

2.   Payment for inventory (parts or merchandise) is an expense---money going out of a firm. Revenues don't come back into the firm until the finished product is produced or the merchandise is sold. In the meantime, other bills will likely have to be paid. So, if a firm carries too much inventory than it has too much money wrapped up in that inventory (parts or merchandise). A firm will likely experience a cash flow problem---an inability to pay its bills. If it gets too bad, the firm will have to borrow to keep the business going. That can be expensive, adding to the cash-flow problem. If the problem persists, banks may be reluctant to loan the firm money. If that happens, then the firm must sell off its inventory; possibly at a loss. Inventory control is vital to avoid cash-flow problems which can result in business failure.

3.   A quality labor force is extremely important in a manufacturer's plant location decision. Indeed, evidence shows this is one of the single most important factors in the location decision---more important than the wage rate itself. (Businesses are willing to pay higher wages if the productivity of workers more than compensates for those high wages.) Indeed, the evidence shows that most manufacturing facilities are most interested in a broad-based, high quality, "lower-half" of the labor force---workers on the lower half of

the spectrum. Most manufacturing firms need workers who possess the basic skills---the ability to read, write, concentrate, do basic math, and are trainable. What is the relevance for public policy-makers whom are interested in attracting jobs to their area? It is absolutely essential that the community provide a sound public education system to its citizens.

4.   A JIT inventory control system can enable management to pinpoint problems in the production process when the system does not run smoothly. This, in turn, can enable management to correct the problems thereby giving rise to higher quality production over time. (The problem is that this may be expensive due to down time on the production floor until the problems are worked out.)

Crossword Puzzle

CHAPTER 12

Chapter 13

Designing and Implementing Customer-Driven Marketing Strategies

"...[there are] four elements of the marketing mix---product, pricing, distribution, and promotional strategy..." (274)

KEY CONCEPTS

Target market	The group of people toward whom a firm markets its goods, services, or ideas with a strategy designed to satisfy their specific meeds and preferences. (274)
Marketing mix	A blending of the four strategy elements of marketing decision making---product, price, distribution, and promotion---to satisfy chosen consumer segments. (275)
Product	A bundle of physical, service, and symbolic attributes designed to satisfy consumer wants. (275)
Product line	A series of related products. (277)
Product life cycle	Introduction, growth, maturity, and decline. (277)
Price	The exchange value of a good or service. (280)
Distribution channels	The paths that products---and title to them---follow from producer to consumer. (280)
Physical distribution	The actual movement of products from the producer to the user. (280)
Marketing intermediaries	The channel members that operate between the producer and the consumer or business user . (Also called middlemen.) (281)
Wholesaling intermediaries	Distribution-channel members that sell primarily to retailers, other wholesalers, or business users. (281)

258

Retailers	Distribution-channel members that sell goods and services to individuals for their own use rather than for resale. (281)
Customer service standards	Measure of quality of service a firm provides for its customers. (285)
Promotional mix	The firm's combination of personal selling and nonpersonal selling designed to achieve promotional objectives. (286)
Personal selling	A promotional presentation made on a person-to-person basis with a potential buyer. (286)
Nonpersonal selling	Advertising, sales promotion, and public relations. (286)
Advertising	A paid, nonpersonal sales communications usually directed at a large number of customers. (286)
Sales promotion	A form of promotion designed to increase sales through one-time selling efforts, such as displays, trade shows, or special events. (287)
Public relations	An organization's communications with its customers, vendors, news media, employees, stockholders, government, and the general public. (287)
Pushing strategy	A sales-oriented approach where the product is marketed to wholesalers and retailers in the distribution channels. (288)
Pulling strategy	An attempt to generate customer demand for the product, primarily through advertising and sales promotion appeals. (288)

Name:_____**Professor:**_____

Section:_____**Date:**_____

ANALYSIS OF LEARNING GOALS

Learning Goal 13.1
Explain what a product is and list the components of product strategy. (275)

Describe

Explain what a product is and list the components of product strategy.

Learning Goal 13.2
Identify the classification of consumer products, business products, and services. (275-277)

Multiple Choice

1. Consumer goods:
   a. are purchased by ultimate consumers for their own use.
   b. are purchased for use either directly or indirectly in the production of other goods for resale.
   c. can be classified as installations, accessory equipment, component parts and materials, raw materials and supplies.
   d. all of the above.

2. Consumer goods can be classified as:
   a. convenience products.
   b. shopping products.
   c. specialty products.
   d. all of the above.

3. A convenience product is a product purchased by consumers:
   a. only after the consumer has compared competing products in competing stores.
   b. frequently and with little effort.
   c. after the purchaser is familiar with the item, considers it to have few suitable substitutes, and is willing to make a special effort to obtain it.
   d. for further processing or for resale.

4. Product strategy:
   a. entails a decision by a firm whether to purchase capital items, accessory equipment, or component parts.
   b. is the decision by a firm concerning the amount of raw materials to purchase.
   c. includes decisions by a firm about package design, brand name, trademarks, warranties, product image, new-product development, and customer service associated with the product it produces.
   d. is the decision by a consumer concerning whether to buy a specialty product or a shopping product.

Fill in the Table

Fill in the table indicating the relationship between consumer products classification and marketing strategy.

Marketing Strategy Factor	Convenience Product	Shopping Product	Specialty Product
Store Image (Important, or unimportant?)			
Price (High, or low?)			
Promotion (By manufacturer or retailer?)			
Distribution Channel (Many, or few wholesalers and retailers?)			
Number of Retail Outlets (Many, or few?)			

Learning Goal 13.3
Discuss the product mix and the stages of the product life cycle. (277-280)

Listing

List the four stages of the product life cycle as described by the following statements.

Introductory Stage   1.   The firm attempts to elicit demand for the product.

Growth Stage   2.   In this stage, sales climb, and the company earns profits.

Maturity Stage   3.   In this stage, sales reach a saturation level.

Decline Stage   4.   In this stage, both sales and profits wane.

262

List the strategies that marketers use to extend the product life cycle as described by the following examples.

Increasing the frequency of use 5.   Persuading homeowners that they need to have smoke alarms.

Adding new users 6.   Gerber products increased the size of its babyfood market by creating specialty foods for foreign consumers.

Finding new uses for the product 7.   Arm & Hammer baking soda is advertised as being useful as a refrigerator freshener.

Changing the package size, shape 8.   Timex Corporation, maker of wristwatches, designs a new wristwatch for kids featuring a favorite comic character on the face.

Learning Goal 13.4
Describe the importance of pricing strategy. (280)

Describe

Describe the importance of pricing strategy.

Learning Goal 13.5
Identify the major components of distribution strategy. (280-281)

True or False

T   1.   Another element in the marketing mix is the distribution strategy, which deals with the marketing activities and institutions involved in getting the right good or service to the right place at the right time.

T   2.   The two major components of an organization's distribution strategy are distribution channels and physical distribution.

F   3.   Distribution channels is the actual movement of products from the producer to the consumer.

F   4.   Distribution channels covers a broad range of activities, including customer service, transportation, inventory control, materials handling, order processing, and warehousing.

Learning Goal 13.6
Outline the various types of distribution channels,
and discuss the factors that influence channel selection. (281-285)

True or False

T   1.   Distribution channels vary in length; products that are complex, expensive, custom made, or perishable generally move through shorter distribution channels.

T   2.   Selecting a distribution channel involves consideration of various factors, including product, producer, competition, and market---where the market may be the most important consideration in choosing a distribution channel.

F   3.   Marketing intermediaries are distribution-channel members that sell only goods and services to individuals for their own use rather than for resale.

T   4.   Retailers are distribution-channel members that sell goods and services to individuals for their own use rather than for resale.

Learning Goal 13.7
Explain the importance of customer service. (285-286)

---

1.   What is customer-service standards? How important are they?

2.   What are some components of good customer service?

Learning Goal 13.8
Explain how advertising, sales promotion, and public relations are used in promotional strategy, and identify the factors that influence the selection of a promotional mix. (286-289)

Multiple Choice

1.   Promotional strategy is:
      a.   the final marketing mix element.
      b.   the function of informing, persuading, and influencing a consumer decision.
      c.   as important to non-profit organizations as it is for profit-oriented organizations.
      d.   all of the above.

---

2.   The promotional mix is:
    a.   the firm's combination of personal selling and nonpersonal selling designed to achieve promotional objectives.
    b.   a paid, nonpersonal sales communications usually directed at a large number of customers.
    c.   always the same for all products.
    d.   a promotional presentation made on a person-to-person basis with a potential buyer.

3.   A form of promotion designed to increase sales through one-time selling efforts, such as displays, trade shows, or special events is known as:
    a.   personal selling
    b.   nonpersonal selling.
    c.   a sales promotion.
    d.   public relations.

4.   Which of the following statements is true about the promotional mix?
    a.   The first decision necessary in the development of a promotional mix is whether to use advertising and/or personal selling.
    b.   Sales promotions and public relations efforts are determined after the advertising and/or personal selling decision is made
    c.   The promotional mix decision is determined by the type of product (business or consumer) being sold, the value of the product, and the timing of its use.
    d.   All of the above.

Learning Goal 13.9
Discuss the factors that influence international promotion. (289)

Describe
Discuss the factors that influence international promotion.

Name:_____ **Professor:**_____
Section:_____ **Date:**_____

SELF REVIEW
True or False

___F___ 1. Product strategy is primarily concerned with producing a good or service efficiently.

___T___ 2. Classifying consumer goods is a useful tool in the development of effective marketing strategies.

___F___ 3. The order of a typical product life cycle is: introduction, maturity, growth and then the decline of the product.

___T___ 4. Marketing strategies designed to extend the product life cycle include increasing the frequency of use, adding new users, finding new uses for the product, and changing the package size, label, or product quality.

___T___ 5. An item is worth only what someone is willing to pay for it.

___T___ 6. Research shows that the consumer's perception of product quality is related closely to the item's price: the higher the price, the better its perceived quality.

___T___ 7. The two major components of an organization's distribution strategy are distribution channels and physical distribution.

___F___ 8. Inexpensive or standardized products typically are sold through shorter distribution channels.

___F___ 9. Customer service standards have been falling recently in the United States.

___F___ 10. Promotional strategy is the final marketing mix element which involves the function of informing, persuading, and influencing a consumer decision.

___F___ 11. A pulling strategy is a sales-oriented approach where the product is marketed to wholesalers and retailers in the distribution channels.

___F___ 12. Developing the right promotional mix is one of the easiest tasks confronting marketers.

___F___ 13. Effective strategies for promoting products to Japanese audiences are guaranteed to work in other countries because the Japanese have high standards for quality.

268

Multiple Choice

1.   Which of the following statements is true?
  a.   Consumer goods can be can be classified as convenience products, shopping products, or specialty products.
  b.   Product strategy includes decisions by a firm about package design, brand name, trademarks, warranties, product image, new-product development, and customer service associated with the product it produces.
  c.   Business goods are purchased for use either directly or indirectly in the production of other goods for resale.
  d.   Services can be classified as either consumer or business services.
  e.   All of the above.

2.   A marketing strategy in which store image is important, the price is high, promotion is undertaken by the manufacturer and retailers, where there are very few wholesalers and retailers, and where there are a very small number of retail outlets characterizes a:
  a.   business good.
  b.   specialty consumer good
  c.   shopping consumer good.
  d.   convenience consumer good.
  e.   business capital item.

3.   The stage of the product life cycle in which sales reach a saturation level is the:
  a.   growth stage.
  b.   maturity stage.
  c.   decline stage.
  d.   introduction stage.
  e.   research stage.

4.   Which of the following products would be considered in the introduction stage?
  a.   Wireless battery-operated personal computers.
  b.   non-alcoholic brews.
  c.   telephone-answering machines.
  d.   wood stoves.
  e.   musical compact disks.

---

5. Which of the following statements is true about distribution strategy?
   a. Distribution strategy is the least important of all marketing strategies in the marketing mix.
   b. Distribution strategy deals with the marketing activities and institutions involved in getting the right good or service to the firm's customers.
   c. The two major components of the distribution strategy is pricing and promoting the good or service appropriately.
   d. Distribution channels are the actual movement of products to the user.
   e. Physical distribution refers to the paths that products---and title to them---follow from producer to consumer.

6. Which of the following statement is true concerning distribution channels?
   a. Distribution channels are approximately the same in length.
   b. Products that are complex, expensive, custom made, or perishable generally move through shorter distribution channels.
   c. Wholesaling intermediaries are distribution-channel members that sell primarily to retailers, other wholesalers, or business users.
   d. Business goods and services typically move through longer distribution channels.
   e. All of the above.

7. The promotional strategy:
   a. is the first marketing mix element which must be considered by a firm.
   b. is the function of informing, persuading, and influencing a consumer decision.
   c. important to for-profit organizations but not non-profit organizations.
   d. must first determine the sales promotion and public relations efforts then decide the extent to which the firm will advertise and/or undertake personal selling.
   e. all of the above.

8. Which of the following statements is true concerning the promotional strategy of a company?
   a. The promotional mix is the firm's combination of personal selling and nonpersonal selling designed to achieve promotional objectives.
   b. Personal selling is a form of promotion designed to increase sales through one-time selling efforts, such as displays, trade shows, or special events.
   c. Public relations is a sales-oriented approach where the product is marketed to wholesalers and retailers in the distribution channels.
   d. Advertising is a promotional presentation made on a person-to-person basis with a potential buyer.
   e. Pushing strategy is an attempt to generate customer demand for the product, primarily through advertising and sales promotion appeals.

270

9.	Which of the following is a component of the promotional mix?
	a.	Personal selling.
	b.	Advertising.
	c.	Sales promotion.
	d.	Public relations.
	e.	All of the above.

10.	Which of the following is a question which a marketer will likely ask in determining the appropriate promotional mix?
	a.	What is the target market?
	b.	What is the value of the product?
	c.	What time frame is involved?
	d.	Should the promotional budget be spent on advertising or personal selling?
	e.	All of the above.

11.	International promotional strategies:
	a.	are the same world-wide.
	b.	are different only in terms of the language in which products are promoted.
	c.	are different due to language and cultural differences.
	d.	are not effected by differences in laws within different countries.
	e.	are different only in terms of language and media availability.

Name:_____**Professor:**_____

Section:_____**Date:**_____

APPLICATION EXERCISES

1.   Suppose a firm has developed a new product. The company is so excited about its new product that it exclaims, "this good will sell itself." Does this mean that a promotional strategy is not important? Generally, what kind of marketing strategy would you recommend for this good?

2.   Advertising agencies often argue that "advertising doesn't cost; it pays!". What do they mean? Is that possible? Generally, what is the recommended amount of advertising dollars which should be spent by a firm?

272

3.   Assume you are a manufacturer of a good which is in the declining stage of its product life cycle. What type of strategies would you recommend to extend its life?

4.   What is the likely relationship between the degree of competition and customer service?

Name:_____**Professor:**_____

Section:_____**Date:**_____

CROSSWORD PUZZLE

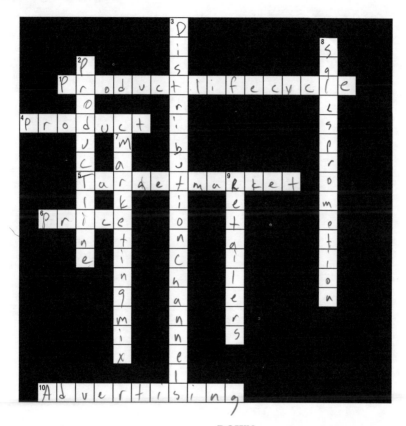

ACROSS

1. Introduction, growth, maturity, and decline. (3 words)

4. A bundle of physical, service, and symbolic attributes designed to satisfy consumer wants.

5. The group of people toward whom a firm markets its goods, services, or ideas with a strategy designed to satisfy their specific needs and preferences. (2 words)

6. The exchange value of a good or service.

10. A paid, nonpersonal sales communications usually directed at a large number of customers.

DOWN

2. A series of related products. (2 words)

3. The paths that products—and title to them—follow from producer to consumer. (2 words)

7. A blending of the four strategy elements of marketing decision making—product, price, distribution, and promotion—to satisfy chosen consumer segments. (2 words)

8. A form of promotion designed to increase sales through one-time selling efforts, such as displays, trade shows, or special events. (2 words)

9. Distribution-channel members that sell goods and services to individuals for their own use rather than for resale.

CHAPTER 13 SOLUTIONS

Analysis of Learning Goals

Learning Goal 13.1

A product is a bundle of physical, service, and symbolic attributes designed to satisfy consumer wants. the product concept includes choosing the brand, product image, warranty, service, packaging, and labeling, in addition to the physical or functional characteristics of the good or service.

Learning Goal 13.2
Multiple Choice

1. a   2. d   3. b   4. c

Fill in the Blank

Marketing Strategy Factor	Convenience Product	Shopping Product	Specialty Product
Store Image (Important, or unimportant?)	Unimportant	Very important	Important
Price (High, or low?)	Low	Relatively high	High
Promotion (By manufacturer or retailer?)	By manufacturer	By manufacturer and retailers	By manufacturer and retailers
Distribution Channel (Many, or few wholesalers and retailers?)	Many wholesalers and retailers	Relatively few wholesalers and retailers	Very few wholesalers and retailers
Number of Retail Outlets (Many, or few?)	Many	Few	Very small number; often one per market area

Learning Goal 13.3
1. Introductory stage
2. Growth stage
3. Maturity stage
4. Decline stage
5. Increasing the frequency of use
6. Adding new users
7. Finding new uses for the product
8. Changing the package size, label, or product quality

Learning Goal 13.4
Price is the exchange value of a good or service. An item is worth only what someone else is willing to pay for it. Pricing strategy deals with the multitude of factors that influence the setting of a price. If a buyer view s a price as too high or too low, the marketer must correct the situation. Price-quality relationships and psychological pricing are important in this regard.

Learning Goal 13.5
1. True   2. True   3. False   4. False

Learning Goal 13.6
1. True   2. True   3. False   4. True

Learning Goal 13.7
1. Customer service is a vital component of marketing strategy. Customer-service standards measure the quality of service a firm provides for its customers and suppliers. The standards set by companies for their suppliers are rising, as U.S. companies gear up to compete more effectively on a global basis.

2. Customer service components include warranty and repair service programs. Products with inadequate service backing quickly disappear from the market as a result of word-of-mouth criticism.

Learning Goal 13.8
1. d
2. a
3. c
4. d

<u>*Learning Goal 13.9*</u>
Cultural sensitivity and good homework are crucial when planning international promotional strategies. Effective strategies for promoting products to U.S. audiences may not work in other countries due to differences in media availability, audience characteristics, laws, and product regulations.

Self-Review

True or False

1. F	4. T	7. T	10. T	13. F
2. T	5. T	8. F	11. F	
3. F	6. T	9. F	12. F	

Multiple Choice

1. e	4. a	7. b	10. e
2. b	5. b	8. a	11. c
3. b	6. c	9. e	

Application Exercises

1.   If a good "sells it self" that means that it will likely be well received by the consumer. They will like it. Sales are likely to pick up over a relatively short period of time as consumers become familiar with its existence. However, this does not mean that a promotional strategy is not important. The company would want to expose the product to as many consumers as possible so that it can "sell itself."

Generally, a marketing strategy which maximizes exposure of the new product would be recommended. Obviously the product component of the marketing mix is satisfactory. However, with respect to the pricing component of the marketing mix, it may be wise for the company to price the good at a relatively low level to maximize sales (exposure)---at least at first. Although, the firm may be sacrificing short-run profits, long-run profits will likely be much greater by pricing the good at a relatively low level at first (if indeed the product will sell itself). The distribution component of the marketing mix component will likely be unaffected by the fact the good will "sell itself." The promotional strategy chosen would be extremely important. Every attempt should be made to expose the product (maximize sales) as quickly as possible before a competitor offers a similar product. Sales promotions and advertising would be essential.

278

2.   Advertising, if properly undertaken can increase sales revenues more than it increases a firm's costs. Advertising can increase a firm's profits. A firm should continue to undertake advertising for as long as it generates more sales revenues than it costs the company.

3.   You would want to try to find a way to increase the frequency of its use, add new users, find new uses for the product, and/or change the package size, label, or product quality. Like most marketing activities this requires one to be creative.

4.   The likely relationship between the degree of competition and customer service is an inverse one---the greater the degree of competition the greater the customer service. This is one more reason why we, as consumers, desire competitive markets.

Crossword Puzzle

CHAPTER 13

Accounting and Budgeting

"The availability of jobs and the relatively high starting salaries for talented accounting graduates have made accounting one of the most popular business majors on North American college and university campuses." (186)

KEY CONCEPTS

Accounting	Measuring, interpreting, and communicating financial information to enable others inside and outside the firm to make informed decisions. (296)
Certified public accountants (CPA)	Have demonstrated accounting knowledge by meeting state requirements for education and experience and successfully completing a number of rigorous tests. (299)
Public accountant	Provides accounting services to individuals or business firms for a fee. (299)
Government accountants	Professional accountants who perform services similar to those of private and public accountants. (300)
Accounting process	Procedural cycle, used by accountants in converting individual transactions to financial statements. (300)
Asset	Anything of value owned or leased by a business. (301)
Equity	A claim against the assets of a business. (301)
Liability	Anything owed to creditors. (302)
Owner's equity	Investments in the business made by owners of the firm and retained earnings that were not paid out in dividends. (302)
Accounting equation	Assets are equal to liabilities plus owner's equity. (302)

280

Balance sheet	Financial position of a company as of a particular date. (303)
Income statement	Financial statement summarizing a firm's financial performance in terms of revenues, expenses, and profits over a given time period. (304)
Bottom line	The final figure on the income statement---net income after taxes. (305)
Ratio analysis	One of the most commonly-used tools for (1) measuring the liquidity, profitability, extent of debt financing, and effectiveness of the firm's use of its resources and (2) permitting comparison with other firms and with past performance. (307)
Liquidity ratios	Measure the firm's ability to meet its short-term obligations when they must be paid. (307)
Profitability ratios	Measure the firm's overall financial performance in terms of its ability to generate revenues in excess of operating and other expenses. (307)
Leverage ratios	Measure the extent to which a firm is relying on debt financing. (308)
Activity ratios	Measure the effectiveness of the firm's use of its resources. (308)
Budget	A planning and control tool that reflects expected sales revenues, operating expenses, and cash receipts and outlays. (309)

Name:_____Professor:_____

Section:_____Date:_____

ANALYSIS OF LEARNING GOALS

Learning Goal 14.1

Explain the functions of accounting and its importance to the firm's management and to outside parties, such as investors, creditors, and government agencies. (296-298)

Describe

Explain the functions of accounting and its importance to the firm's management and to outside parties, such as investors, creditors, and government agencies.

Learning Goal 14.2

Identify the three basic business activities involving accounting. (298)

Listing

Identify the three basic business activities involving accounting.

_____ 1. These activities is necessary to start a business and to expand it in the future.

_____ 2. These activities help are involved with providing the assets needed to run the business.

_____ 3. These activities focus on the sale of goods and services and the expenses incurred in operating the business.

Learning Goal 14.3

Contrast the roles played by public, private, government, and not-for-profit accountants. (299-300)

Matching

Match the following types of accountants with their descriptions given below.

a. Public accountants   c. Government accountants
b. Private accountants   d. Not-for-profit accountants

_____1. These accountants are independent organizations or individuals who provide accounting services, such as tax statement preparation, management consulting, and accounting systems design to other firms of individuals for a fee.

_____2. These accountants are primary concerned with how efficiently the organization is accomplishing its objectives under tax-payer scrutiny.

_____3. These accountants are responsible for collecting and recording financial transactions, preparing financial statements, and interpreting them for managers in their own firm.

_____4. These accountants are primary concerned with how efficiently the organization is accomplishing its objectives. This area of accounting is one of the fastest-growing segments of accounting practice.

Learning Goal 14.4

Outline the steps in the accounting process. (300-302)

True or False

_____1. The accounting process involves the recording, classifying, and summarizing of accounting transactions and using this information to produce financial statements for the firm's management and other interested parties.

_____2. Transactions are recorded in journals, posted in ledgers, and then summarized in accounting statements.

_____3.   Computers merely record and organize data for statements.

_____4.   Because of computers, the typical private accountant today spends most time communicating accounting information clearly and effectively for use in decision-making

_____5.   Four fundamental terms are involved in the accounting equation: assets, equities, liabilities, and owners' equity.

_____6.   The accounting equation states that assets equal owners' equity.

_____7.   Owners' equity is anything owed to creditors.

_____8.   Assets represent the investment in the business make by owners of the firm and retained earnings tat were no paid out as dividends.

Learning Goal 14.5
*Explain the functions of the balance sheet and the income statement
and identify their major components.* (302-307)

True or False

_____1.   The income statement shows the financial position of a company as of a particular date.

_____2.   The balance sheet shows the operation of a firm over a specified period of time.

_____3.   The income statement focuses on the firm's activities---its revenues and expenditures---and the firm's profit or loss during the period.

_____4.   The major components of the income statement are revenues, cost of goods sold, expenses, and profits or losses.

_____5.   The three major classifications on the income statement represent the components of the accounting equation: assets, liabilities, and owners' equity.

_____6.   The statement of cash flows provides investors and creditors with relevant information about a firm's cash receipts and cash payments (its cash flow) during an accounting period.

284

Learning Goal 14.6
Discuss how the major financial ratios are used in analyzing a firm's financial strengths and weaknesses. (307-309)

Describe

What purpose do financial ratios serve?

Matching

Match the following financial ratios with the statements below.

a. Liquidity analysis   c. Leverage ratios
b. Profitability ratios   d. Activity ratios

_____1. Measure the effectiveness of the firm's use of its resources.

_____2. Measure the extent to which a firm is relying on debt financing.

_____3. Measure the firm's overall financial performance in terms of its ability to generate revenues in excess of operating and other expenses.

_____4. Measure the firm's ability to meet its short-term obligations when they must be paid.

Learning Goal 14.7
Explain the role of budgets in business. (309-310)

Describe

Explain the role of budgets in business.

Learning Goal 14.8
Explain the impact of exchange rates on international accounting and the importance of uniform financial statements for firms engaged in international business. (310-311)

1.   What is an exchange rate?

286

2.   How do exchange rates affect firms involved in international markets?

Name:_____**Professor:**_____

Section:_____**Date:**_____

SELF REVIEW

True or False

_____1.   Accountants must accomplish three major tasks: scorekeeping, calling attention to problems and opportunities, and aiding in decision making.

_____2.   Accounting plays a key role in all three basic activities of business: financing, investing, and operating activities.

_____3.   A Certified Public Accountant is an accountant who works for the government.

_____4.   A cost accountant is concerned with minimizing taxes paid and is in charge of the firm's federal, state, county, and city tax returns.

_____5.   The accounting equation states that assets are equal to liabilities plus owners' equity.

_____6.   Owners' equity equal assets minus liabilities.

_____7.   An asset is anything of value owned or leased by a business.

_____8.   A balance sheet shows the financial position of a firm as of a particular date in time; an income statement shows the operations of a firm over a period of time.

_____9.   The statement of cash flows indicates a company's ability to pay its bills on time.

_____10.   The three major classifications on the balance sheet represent the components of the accounting equation: assets, liabilities, and owners' equity.

_____11.   Ratio analysis is one of the most commonly-used tools for (1) measuring the liquidity, profitability, extent of debt financing, and effectiveness of the firm's use of its resources and (2)permitting comparison with other firms and with past performance.

_____12.   The acid-test ratio measures the ability of a firm to meet its debt on short notice.

_____13.   A firm's budget is usually established on a five-year basis.

_____14.   An exchange rate is the rate at which a country's currency can be exchanged for other currencies or gold.

288

Multiple Choice

1.   Accountants:
     a.   measure, interpret, and communicate financial information to parties inside and outside the firm for effective decision making.
     b.   are responsible for gathering, recording, and interpreting financial information to management.
     c.   provide financial information on the status and operation of the firm for use by such outside parties as government agencies and potential investors and lenders.
     d.   all of the above.
     e.   none of the above.

2.   The accounting activity which focuses on the sale of goods and services and the expenses incurred in operating the business are known as the:
     a.   financing activities of accounting
     b.   investing activities of accounting
     c.   operating activities of accounting
     d.   liquidating activities of accounting
     e.   financing activities of accounting

3.   Which of the following statements is true about accountants?
     a.   Public accountants are primarily concerned with how efficiently the organization is accomplishing its objectives; as opposed to how well the organization is earning a profit.
     b.   Private accountants are independent organizations or individuals who provide accounting services, such as tax statement preparation, management consulting, and accounting systems design to other firms of individuals for a fee.
     c.   Public accountants provide accounting services to individuals or business firms for a fee.
     d.   An internal auditor determines the cost of goods and services, and helps set their prices.
     e.   Tax accountants examine a company's books for accuracy and to ensure the firm is in compliance with government laws and regulations.

4. Which of the following statements is true concerning the accounting process.

   a. The accounting process involves the recording, classifying, and summarizing of accounting transactions and using this information to produce financial statements for the firm's management and other interested parties.

   b. Transactions are recorded in journals, posted in ledgers, and then summarized in accounting statements.

   c. In order to provide reliable, consistent, and unbiased information to decision makers accountants follow guidelines, or standards known as "generally accepted accounting principles" (GAAP).

   d. Two accounting statements form the foundation of the entire accounting system: the balance sheet and the income statement.

   e. all of the above.

5. In the accounting equation:

   a. assets are anything owed to creditors.

   b. assets equal liabilities plus owners' equity

   c. assets equal liabilities minus owners' equity

   d. Owners' equity is anything owed to creditors.

   e. liabilities are anything of value owned or leased by the firm.

6. Which of the following statements is true?

   a. Owners' equity equal assets minus liabilities.

   b. Owners' equity represents investments in the business made by owners of the firm and retained earnings that were not paid out in dividends.

   c. Assets are anything of value owned or leased by a firm.

   d. Equity is a claim against the assets of a business.

   e. All of the above.

7. The balance sheet:

   a. shows the financial position of a company as of a particular date.

   b. shows the operation of a firm over a specified period of time.

   c. focuses on the firm's activities---its revenues and expenditures---and the firm's profit or loss incurred over a period of time.

   d. consists of a statement of revenues, cost of goods sold, expenses, and profits or losses.

   e. indicates that assets plus owners' equity equals liabilities.

8. The income statement:
   a. shows the operation of a firm over a specified period of time.
   b. focuses on the firm's activities---its revenues and expenditures---and the firm's profit or loss during the period.
   c. has as its major components: revenues, cost of goods sold, expenses, and profits or losses.
   d. has a final figure---net income after taxes---which is commonly referred to as "the bottom line."
   e. all of the above.

9. A measure of the extent to which a firm is relying on debt financing can be analyzed in terms of:
   a. liquidity ratios.
   b. profitability ratios.
   c. activity ratios.
   d. leverage ratios.
   e. budgeting ratios.

10. To determine a firm's ability to pay its bills on time, an investor would want to analyze:
    a. liquidity ratios.
    b. profitability ratios.
    c. activity ratios.
    d. leverage ratios.
    e. budgeting ratios.

11. Budgets are:
    a. the quantification of the firm's plans for a specified future period.
    b. financial guidelines for future periods reflecting expected sales revenues, operating expenses, and/or cash receipts and outlays.
    c. the representation of management's expectations about future occurrences based on plans that have been made.
    d. an important planning and control tool because they provide standards against which actual performance can be compared.
    e. all of the above.

12. Which of the following statements is true regarding exchange rates and firms involved in international markets.
    a. The daily changes in exchange rates do not affect the accounting entries for sales and purchase transactions of firms involved in international markets.
    b. The daily changes in exchange rates always create a loss for the company because of the greater uncertainty they create.
    c. There is no need for financial statements to be translated into the currency of the country in which the parent company resides.
    d. The International Accounting Standards Committee was established to provide world-wide consistency in financial reporting practices and comparability and uniformity of international accounting standards.
    e. Exchange rates are held constant by governments.

13. Which of the following statements is true?
    a. The inventory turnover ratio equals cost of goods sold divided by average inventory, and indicates the number of times merchandise moves through the business.
    b. The debt-to-owners' equity equals owners' equity divided by total liabilities, and indicates the extent to which a firm is relying on debt financing.
    c. Earnings per share equal common shares outstanding divided by net income after taxes.
    d. Return on assets equal net sales divided by net income.
    e. Return on equity equals total owners' equity divided by net income.

14. Which of the following statements is *false*?
    a. The current ratio equals current assets divided by current liabilities.
    b. The acid-test ratio equals quick assets divided by current liabilities, and the traditional rule of thumb is that it should be at least equal to one.
    c. The debt-to-owners' equity ratio of less than one would indicate the firm is relying more on debt financing than owners' equity.
    d. A current ratio of 2 to 1 is considered financially satisfactory.
    e. The acid-test ratio measures the ability of the firm to meet its debt on short notice.

Name:_____Professor:_____

Section:_____Date:_____

APPLICATION EXERCISES

1.   Use the accounts below to answer the following questions.

Net Sales   Accounts receivable   Advertising expense
Common stock   Equipment   Marketable securities
Salaries   Retained earnings   Long-term notes payable
Cash   Inventory   Rent

   a.   Which of these would be considered a current asset? Why?

   b.   Which of these would be considered a fixed asset? Why?

   c.   Which of these would be considered a current liability? Why?

   d.   Which of these would be considered a long-term liability? Why?

   e.   Which of these would be considered owners' equity?

   f.   Which of these would be considered a revenue?

   g.   Which of these would be considered an expense?

294

2.   Indicate the ratio that would provide information on:
       a.   A firm's ability to meet short-term obligations.

       b.   A firm's ability to pay current debts.

       c.   A firm's ability to pay current debts on short notice.

       d.   A firm's overall financial performance.

       e.   The amount of profits earned for each share of common stock outstanding.

       f.   Net income compared to sales.

       g.   Owners' equity.

       h.   A firm's use of its resources.

       i.   The number of times merchandise moves through the business.

       j.   The extent to which a firm relies on financing.

       k.   The percentage of owners' investments to debt financing.

3.   At the end of the year, Pat Myers, Inc. showed the following balances on accounts:

Land.. $ 70,000
Buildings.. 320,000
Inventory.. 110,000
Cash... 20,000
Accounts payable.................................. 120,000
Marketable securities............................. 42,000
Retained earnings................................. 392,000
Common Shares..................................... 80,000
(40,000 shares @ $2)
Notes payable..................................... 120,000
Equipment... 60,000

a.   Prepare a balance sheet for Pat Myers, Inc.
b.   Calculate the current ratio, acid-test ratio, and debt-to-owners' equity ratio. What conclusions can be drawn from these ratios?

Name:_____Professor:_____
Section:_____Date:_____

CROSSWORD PUZZLE

ACROSS

1. Provides accounting services to individuals or business firms for a fee. (2 words)

3. Anything of value owned or leased by a business.

6. Investments in the business made by owners of the firm and retained earnings that were not paid out in dividends. (2 words)

9. These measure the extent to which a firm is relying on debt financing. (2 words)

DOWN

2. A planning and control tool that reflects expected sales revenues, operating expenses, and cash receipts and outlays.

4. One of the most commonly-used tools for (1) measuring the liquidity, profitability, extent of debt financing, and effectiveness of the firm's use of its resources and (2) permitting comparison with other firms and with past performance. (2 words)

5. Financial statement summarizing a firm's financial performance in terms of revenues, expenses, and profits over a period of time. (2 words)

7. Financial position as of a particular date. (2 words)

8. A claim against the assets of a business.

10. The final figure on the income statement—net income after taxes. (2 words)

CHAPTER 14 SOLUTIONS

Analysis of Learning Goals

Learning Goal 14.1

Accountants measure, interpret, and communicate financial information to parties inside and outside the firm for effective decision making. They are responsible for gathering, recording, and interpreting financial information to management. In addition, they provide financial information on the status and operation of the firm for use by such outside parties as government agencies and potential investors and lenders.

Learning Goal 14.2

1.   Financing activities
2.   Investing activities
3.   Operating activities

Learning Goal 14.3

1. a   2. c   3. d   4. b

Learning Goal 14.4

1. True
2. True
3. False
4. True
5. True
6. False
7. False
8. False

Learning Goal 14.5

1. False
2. False
3. True
4. True
5. False
6. True

300

Learning Goal 14.6
Describe
Financial ratios assist managers and others outside the firm in comparing the firm's performance over time and with other firms in the industry, or against some standard. This is known as ratio analysis.

Matching
1. d
2. c
3. b
4. a

Learning Goal 14.7
Budgets are financial guidelines for future periods reflecting expected sales revenues, operating expenses, and/or cash receipts and outlays. They represent management's expectations of future occurrences based on plans that have been made. They serve as important planning and control tools by providing standards against which actual performance can be compared.

Learning Goal 14.8
1. An exchange rate is the rate at which a country's currency can be exchanged for other currencies or gold.

2. The daily changes in exchange rates affects the accounting entries for sales and purchase transactions of firms involved in international markets. They create either a loss or a gain for the company, depending on whether they increase or decrease. Financial statements must be translated into the currency of the country in which the parent company resides. The International Accounting Standards Committee was established to provide world-wide consistency in financial reporting practices and comparability and uniformity of international accounting standards.

Self-Review

True or False

1. T	4. F	7. T	10. T	13. F
2. T	5. T	8. T	11. T	14. T
3. F	6. T	9. T	12. T	

Multiple Choice

1. d	4. e	7. a	10. a	13. a
2. c	5. b	8. e	11. e	14. c
3. c	6. e	9. d	12. d	

Application Exercises

1. a. Cash, accounts receivable, inventory, and marketable securities would all be considered current assets. This is because current assets are cash and other liquid assets that can or will be converted to cash or used within one year.

    b. Equipment is the only fixed asset on this list. This is because fixed assets are relatively permanent plant, property, and equipment expected to be used for periods longer than one year.

    c. Salaries, advertising expenses and rent accrued are the current liabilities. Current liabilities are claims by creditors that are to be repaid within one year.

    d. Long-term notes payable are the only long-term liability on this list. Long-term liabilities are debts that come due one year or more after the date of the balance sheet.

    e. Common stock and retained earnings are the owners' equity because owners' equity are claims of the proprietor, partners, or stockholders (stockholders in this case) against the assets of the a firm; the excess of assets over liabilities.

    f. Net sales, and interest from marketable securities (and retained earnings if it is earning interest) constitutes the revenue.

    g. The expenses include: salaries, advertising expenses, interest on long-term notes payable, and rent (as well as depreciation on the equipment).

2. a. The liquidity ratios (the current and acid-test ratios).
    b. The current ratio (one of the liquidity ratios).
    c. The acid-test (or quick) ratio (one of the liquidity ratios).
    d. The profitability ratios (earnings per share, return on sales, and return on equity).
    e. The earnings per share ratio (one of the profitability ratios).
    f. The return on sales ratios (one of the profitability ratios).
    g. The return on equity ratios (one of the profitability ratios).
    h. The activity ratios (for example, the inventory turnover ratio).
    i. The inventory turnover ratio (one of the activity ratios).
    j. The leverage ratios(for example, the debt-to-owners' equity ratio).
    k. The debt-to-owners' equity ratio (one of the leverage ratios).

302

3.   a.

Pat Myers, Inc.
Balance Sheet

ASSETS

Current Assets

Cash	$110.000	
Marketable Securities	42,000	
Inventory	110,000	
Total Current Assets		*$262,000*

Fixed Assets

Land	$ 70,000	
Buildings	320,000	
Equipment	60,000	
Total fixed Assets		*$450,000*
Total Assets		**$712,000**

LIABILITIES AND OWNERS' EQUITY

Current Liabilities

Accounts Payable	$120,000	
Total Current liabilities		*$120,000*

Long-Term Liabilities

Notes Payable	$120,000	
Total Long-Term liabilities		*$120,000*
Total Liabilities		*$240,000*

Owners' Equity

Common Shares	$ 80,000	
(40,000 shares @ $2)		
Retained Earnings	392,000	
Total Owners' Equity		*$472,000*
Total Liabilities &Owners' Equity		**$712,000**

b.   **Current ratio** = $\dfrac{\text{Current Assets}}{\text{Current Liabilities}}$ = $\dfrac{\$262{,}000}{\$120{,}000}$ =   2.18

Because, in general, a current ratio of 2 to 1 is considered financially satisfactory, then Pat Myers, Inc. appears to be in good shape to meet its short-term obligations.

Acid-test ratio = $\dfrac{\text{Quick Assets}}{\text{Current Liabilities}}$ = $\dfrac{\text{Cash and Marketable Securities}}{\text{Current Liabilities}}$

= $\dfrac{\$152{,}000}{\$120{,}000}$ = 1.26

Because, in general, an adequate acid-test ratio of 1 to 1 is adequate, and Pat Myers, Inc. is better than that, then it appears that the company is in good shape to meet its debt on short notice. However, a word of caution: ratios are most meaningful when compared with industry averages---what is typical for the industry.

Debt-to-owners' equity ratio = $\dfrac{\text{Total Liabilities}}{\text{Owners' Equity}}$ = $\dfrac{\$240{,}000}{\$472{,}000}$ = 50.8%

Because, in general, a debt-to-equity ratio of greater than 1 would indicate the firm is relying more on debt financing than the owners' equity, it is clear that the owners of Pat Myers, Inc. have invested more than the total amount of liabilities shown on the firm's balance sheet. The firm is not too much in debt.

Pat Myers, Inc. looks like a solid company based on these ratios. However, be careful not to judge a company based on ratio analysis alone.

Crossword Puzzle

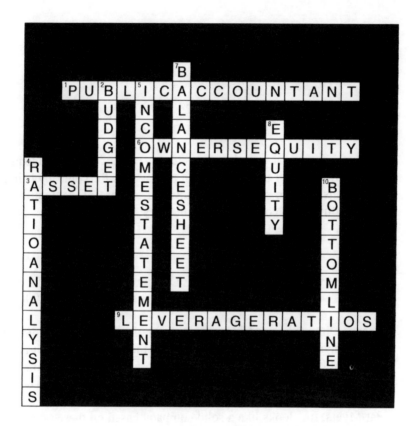

CHAPTER 14

Chapter 15

Banking and Financial Management

"More and more frequently, businesses designate a financial manager to be responsible for both meeting expenses and increasing profits for the firm's stockholders." (318)

KEY CONCEPTS

Finance	Planning, obtaining, and managing the company's use of funds to accomplish its objectives most effectively. (318)
Financial managers	Those responsible for developing and implementing the firm's financial plan and for determining the most appropriate sources and uses of funds. (319)
Risk-return-tradeoff	Balance between the risk of an investment and it potential gain. (319)
Financial plan	Document that specifies the funds needed by a firm for a period of time, indicates the timing of inflows and outflows, and indicates the most appropriate sources and uses of funds. (319)
Financial control	A process that periodically checks actual revenues, costs, and expenses against the forecasts. (319)
Money	Anything generally accepted as a means of paying for goods and services. (320)
Near-money	Assets that are almost as liquid as cash or checking accounts but cannot be used directly as a medium of exchange. (321)
Debt capital	Funds obtained through borrowing. (323)
Equity capital	Funds provided by the firm's owners by reinvesting earnings, making additional contributions, liquidating assets, issuing stock to the general public, or by soliciting contributions from venture capitalists. (323)

306

Bonds	Certificates of indebtedness sold to raise long-term funds for corporations or government agencies. (324)
Leverage	A technique of increasing the rate of return on investment through the use of borrowed funds. (325)
Commercial banks	Profit-making businesses that hold the deposits of individuals, business firms, and not-for-profit organizations in the form of checking or savings accounts and use these funds to make loans to individuals and businesses. (326)
Electronic fund transfer systems (EFTS)	Computerized systems for conducting financial transactions electronically. (327)
Savings and loan association (S&L)	A thrift institution offering both savings and checking accounts and using most of its funds to make home mortgage loans. (328)
Savings banks	State-chartered banks with operations similar to those of S&Ls. (Also known as Mutual Savings banks.) (328)
Credit union	A member-owned financial cooperative that pays interest to depositors, offers share draft accounts, and makes short-term loans and some home-mortgage loans. (328)
Federal Reserve System	A network of 12 district banks, controlled by a board of governors, that regulates banking in the United States. (329)
Foreign exchange market	Purchases and sales of one nation's currency are made for that of another country. (330)
Federal Deposit Insurance Corporation (FDIC)	Insures depositors' accounts up to a maximum of $100,000 per account and sets requirements for sound banking practices. (331)
Bank examiner	A trained representative who inspects the financial records and management practices of each federally insured financial institution. (331)

Name:_____Professor:_____
Section:_____Date:_____

ANALYSIS OF LEARNING GOALS

Learning Goal 15.1
Identify the functions performed by a firm's financial manager. (319-320)

Multiple Choice

1.   Financial managers:
    a.   develop and implement a firm's financial plan.
    b.   are responsible for raising and spending money.
    c.   help determine the most appropriate sources and uses of funds.
    d.   all of the above.

2.   Which of the following statements is true?
    a.   Risk is the gain or loss that results from an investment over a specified period.
    b.   Loss is the uncertainty of an investment.
    c.   The financial manager strives to maximize the wealth of a firm's stockholders by striking a balance between the risk of an investment and its potential gain.
    d.   In reality, few financial managers perform the risk-return balancing act.

3.   The risk-return tradeoff implies that usually:
    a.   the lower the potential return from an investment, the greater the risk.
    b.   the greater the potential return from an investment, the greater the risk.
    c.   the greater the potential return from an investment, the lower the risk.
    d.   risk and return are not related.

4.   Which of the following statements is true about a financial plan?
    a.   It is based on a forecast of expenditures and receipts for a specified period.
    b.   It and reflects the timing of cash inflows and outflows, and it indicates the most appropriate sources and uses of funds.
    c.   A good financial plan also involves financial control, a process that periodically checks actual revenues, costs, and expenses against the forecasts.
    d.   All of the above.

308

Learning Goal 15.2
*Describe the characteristics a good form of money should have
and list the functions of money.* (320-321)

Describe

1.　What is money?

2.　What are the characteristics of money in order for it to serve its functions?

Listing

List the three functions of money as described by the following statements.

<u>Medium of exchange</u> 1.　It serves primarily as a means of facilitating exchange and eliminating the need for a barter system.

<u>Store of value</u> 2.　It is a way of keeping accumulated wealth until it is needed to make new purchases.

<u>Unit of account</u> 3.　It acts as a common denominator for measuring the value of all goods and services.

Learning Goal 15.3
Distinguish between money (M1) and near-money (M2). (321)

True or False

T 1.   *M1* equals coins, paper money, traveler's checks, demand deposits (checking accounts), interest-bearing NOW (negotiable order of withdrawal) accounts, and credit union share draft accounts.

F 2.   Near-money is money in a checking account.

T 3.   Near-money is assets that are almost as liquid as cash or checking accounts but cannot be used directly as a medium of exchange.

T 4.   Examples of near money include time deposits (savings accounts), government bonds, and money market mutual funds.

F 5.   The categories of near-money are commonly referred to as *M1*.

Learning Goal 15.4
Explain how a firm uses funds. (321-323)

---

1.   For what reasons do organizations require funds?

310

2. If a firm has excess cash on hand what will a financial manager likely do with these funds? Why?

Learning Goal 15.5

Compare the two major categories of sources of funds. (323)

True or False

_F_ 1. Equity capital represents funds obtained through borrowing.

_F_ 2. Debt capital are funds provided by the firm's owners by reinvesting earnings, making additional contributions, liquidating assets, issuing stock to the general public, or by soliciting contributions from venture capitalists.

_T_ 3. Equity capital can be obtained from revenues from day-to-day operations and from liquidating some of the firm' assets.

_T_ 4. The financial manager's job includes determining the most cost-effective balance between equity and borrowed funds and the proper blending of short- and long-term funds.

Learning Goal 15.6

Identify likely sources of short-term and long-term funds. (323-326)

Listing

List the four types of short-term funds for business firms as described by the following statements.

Trade credit 1. The major short-term source---making open-account purchases from suppliers.

Unsecured loans 2. A loan in which no collateral is pledged.

---

secured loans _____3. A loan in which collateral is pledged.

_Selling commercial paper_4. Large firms with unquestioned financial stability can raise money from this source.

Describe

1.   Describe the sources of long-term financing.

2.   What is leverage? What could motivate a firm to leverage itself?

Learning Goal 15.7

*Identify the major categories of financial institutions
and the sources and uses of their funds.* (326-329)

Multiple Choice

1. Which of the following is a deposit institution?
    a. A life insurance company
    b. A finance company.
    c. A pension fund.
    d. A commercial bank.

2. Which of the following is a non-deposit institution?
    a. A health insurance company.
    b. A savings and loan.
    c. A credit union.
    d. A commercial bank.

3. The deposit institution which loans most of funds to home buyers is the:
    a. commercial bank.
    b. savings and loan.
    c. credit union.
    d. finance company.

4. A member-owned financial cooperative that pays interest to depositors, offers share draft
    accounts, and makes short-term loans and some home-mortgage loans is a:
    a. commercial bank
    b. savings and loan
    c. credit union
    d. electronic funds transfer system (EFTS).

5. Which of the following statements is true?
    a. State banks are commercial banks chartered by individual states.
    b. More financial institutions are offering electronic funds transfer systems because
        it saves them money.
    c. The term "financial supermarket" describes a growing number of nonbank
        corporations that offer a wide range of financial services, including investments,
        loans, real estate, and insurance.
    d. All of the above.

Learning Goal 15.8

Explain the functions of the Federal Reserve System and the tools it uses to increase or decrease the money supply. (329-331)

True or False

___T___ 1.   The Fed's primary function is to control the supply of credit and money in order to promote economic growth and a stable dollar.

___F___ 2.   Changing the discount rate consists of the Fed buying and selling government bonds.

___T___ 3.   If the Fed wishes to increase the money supply it could reduce the reserve requirement, reduce the discount rate, and/or buy government bonds on the open market.

___T___ 4.   The Fed increases the money supply to stimulate the economy, and decreases the money supply to slow the growth in the economy down.

___T___ 5.   The Fed can lower the exchange value of the dollar by selling dollars and buying foreign currencies in foreign exchange markets.

Learning Goal 15.9

Describe the institutions and practices that regulate bank safety. (331-333)

True or False

___T___ 1.   The FDIC insures depositors' accounts up to a maximum of $100,000 per account and sets requirements for sound banking practices.

___T___ 2.   Deposits at federally insured thrift institutions are covered by the federal Office of Thrift Supervision (OTS) and the Resolution Trust Corporation (RTC).

___T___ 3.   Eighty percent of U.S. credit unions are federally insured by the National Credit Union Share Insurance Fund (NCUSIF).

___T___ 4.   The primary technique for guaranteeing the safety and soundness of commercial banks and thrifts is the use of unannounced inspections of individual institutions at least once a year by bank examiners.

Learning Goal 15.10
Discuss the U.S. financial system in its global context. (333-334)

Describe

Discuss the U.S. financial system in its global context.

Name:_____ Professor:_____
Section:_____ Date:_____

SELF REVIEW

True or False

___T___ 1.　Risk-return-tradeoff is the balance between the risk of an investment and it potential gain.

___T___ 2.　Money is anything which serves the functions of money.

___F___ 3.　If anything is to be considered money it need not serve all three functions of money.

___F___ 4.　*M1* is a broader concept of money than *M2*.

___T___ 5.　Most financial managers will choose to invest the majority of a firm's excess cash in marketable securities.

___F___ 6.　Equity capital represents funds obtained through borrowing.

___T___ 7.　The major short-term source of funds for a company is trade credit, or making open-account purchases from suppliers.

___T___ 8.　Leverage is a technique of trying to increase the rate of return on investment through the use of borrowed funds.

___T___ 9.　A pension fund is a large pool of money set up by a company, union, or not-for-profit organization for the retirement needs of its employees or members.

___F___ 10.　Banks make a profit when the interest rate they charge on loans is less than the interest rate they pay depositors.

___F___ 11.　The Fed could decrease the money supply by decreasing reserve requirements, decreasing the discount rate, or buying government bonds on the open market.

___F___ 12.　Open market operations is the least used tool by the Fed to change the money supply.

___T___ 13.　The Fed should increase the money supply to stimulate the economy, and decrease the money supply to slow the economy down.

___T___ 14.　Deposits up to $100,000 at all commercial banks are insured by the FDIC.

316

Multiple Choice

1. Which of the following questions would likely be asked in developing a financial plan?
    a.   What funds does the firm require during the next period of operations?
    b.   How will the necessary funds be obtained?
    c.   When will more funds be needed?
    d.   All of the above.
    e.   None of the above.

2. Which of the following statements is *false*?
    a.   Financial managers are responsible for developing and implementing the firm's financial plan and for determining the most appropriate sources and uses of funds.
    b.   The financial manager strives to maximize the wealth of a firm's stockholders by striking a balance between the risk of an investment and its potential gain.
    c.   The greater the potential return from an investment, the lower the risk.
    d.   A good financial plan also involves financial control, a process that periodically checks actual revenues, costs, and expenses against the forecasts.
    e.   Risk is the uncertainty of loss; return is the gain or loss that results from an investment over a specified period.

3. If money is operating as a medium of exchange, then it:
    a.   is highly liquid, meaning it can be obtained and disposed of quickly and easily.
    b.   serves as a means of facilitating exchange and eliminating the need for a barter system.
    c.   is a way of keeping accumulated wealth until it is needed to make new purchases.
    d.   acts as a common denominator for measuring the value of all goods and services.
    e.   is divisible, portable and durable.

4. Near-money is:
    a.   *M1*.
    b.   cash.
    c.   money in a checking account.
    d.   is any kind of money which is highly liquid.
    e.   almost as liquid as cash or checking accounts but cannot be used directly as a medium of exchange.

5.	Which of the following statement sis true regarding sources of funds?
	a.	The two sources of funds for a business include debt and equity capital.
	b.	Equity capital represents funds obtained through borrowing.
	c.	Debt capital are funds provided by the firm's owners by reinvesting earnings, making additional contributions, liquidating assets, issuing stock to the general public, or by soliciting contributions from venture capitalists.
	d.	Borrowing is always a better source of funds than raising funds by selling more stock.
	e.	It is always better to borrow long-term rather than short-term.

6.	A difference between debt capital and equity capital, is that equity capital:
	a.	has a maturity date, whereas debt capital does not.
	b.	will be repaid before debt capital in the event of company bankruptcy.
	c.	results in the firm going into debt.
	d.	results in a right to a voice in management.
	e.	results in a contractual obligation by the firm to pay interest before dividends can be paid.

7.	Sources of short-term financing include:
	a.	selling commercial paper.
	b.	selling company assets.
	c.	issuing bonds.
	d.	reinvesting company earnings.
	e.	Loans which can be repaid over one year or longer.

8.	Sources of long-term funds include:
	a.	trade credit.
	b.	selling commercial paper.
	c.	unsecured loans which must be repaid within one year.
	d.	selling stock in the company.
	e.	all of the above.

9.	Leverage:
	a.	is designed to increase interest payments, decrease the reported rate of return, and therefore to decrease taxes.
	b.	can be beneficial to a company as long as the earnings exceed interest payments on borrowed funds.
	c.	increases the flexibility of a firm in future decisions.
	d.	has proven to be successful for virtually every firm who has used it.
	e.	all of the above.

318

10.   Which of the following statements is true?
   a.   Savings banks are State-chartered banks with operations similar to those of S&Ls.
   b.   Savings and loan associations are a thrift institution that offer both savings and checking accounts and use most of their funds to make business loans.
   c.   Savings and loan associations are ember-owned financial cooperatives that pay interest to depositors, offers share draft accounts, and makes short-term loans and some home-mortgage loans.
   d.   Very few financial institutions will be expected to offer electronic funds transfer systems in the future.
   e.   An insurance company is an example of a deposit institution.

11.   The Fed's most powerful tool, and therefore the least used tool to affect the economy, is:
   a.   changing reserve requirements.
   b.   open market operations.
   c.   changing the discount rate.
   d.   changing selective credit controls.
   e.   buying and selling dollars in the foreign exchange markets.

12.   Open market operations is:
   a.   the Fed's buying and selling of government bonds.
   b.   the tool most relied on by the Fed to change the money supply.
   c.   the most flexible tool the Fed has to change the money supply.
   d.   used to increase the money supply by the Fed when it buys government bonds.
   e.   all of the above.

13.   Which of the following statement is true?
   a.   The Fed's primary function is to ensure that banks are following sound banking practices.
   b.   Changing the discount rate consists of the Fed changing the percentage of a bank's checking and saving accounts that must be kept in the bank or on deposit at the local Federal Reserve district bank.
   c.   The Federal Reserve System consists of a network of 50 district banks controlled by the Governors of each state.
   d.   If the Fed wishes to reduce the exchange value of the dollar it would sell dollars or buy foreign currencies in foreign exchange markets.
   e.   When the Fed buys foreign currencies, the effect is like selling government securities, since it decreases the U.S. banking system's reserves.

14. To stimulate the economy, the Fed should:
    a. decrease the money supply by reducing the discount rate, decrease reserve requirements, or buy government bonds on the open market.
    b. decrease the money supply by increasing the discount rate, increase reserve requirements, or sell government bonds on the open market.
    c. increase the money supply by reducing the discount rate, decrease reserve requirements, or buy government bonds on the open market.
    d. increase the money supply by increasing the discount rate, increase reserve requirements, or sell government bonds on the open market.
    e. none of the above.

15. Deposits at federally insured thrift institutions are covered by the:
    a. FDIC.
    b. federal Office of Thrift Supervision (OTS) and the Resolution Trust Corporation (RTC).
    c. by the National Credit Union Share Insurance Fund (NCUSIF).
    d. FSLIC
    e. all of the above.

Name:_____Professor:_____
Section:_____Date:_____

APPLICATION EXERCISES

1.   Consider the information provided in the table below to answer the questions which follow.

Company A		**Company B**	
Common Stock	$ 50,000	Common Stock	$ 200,000
Bonds (at 10% interest)	150,000	Bonds	0
	200,000		200,000
Earnings	40,000	Earnings	40,000
Less bond interest	15,000	Less bond interest	0
	25,000		40,000

   a.   Which of these two companies is leveraged? How do you know?

322

b.	Did leverage work for the company? How do you know?

c.	Now suppose that earnings for both companies fall to $10,000. What's the return to both companies stockholders now? What are some potential problems with the use of leverage to increase the return on investment?

2.   How can an increase in the money supply stimulate the economy?

324

3.   What impact will a change in the value of the dollar in foreign exchange markets have on the relative price of imports coming into the United States and the relative price of American exports? What effect will this have on the amount the U.S. imports and exports? Would an American firm which produces a product for export prefer a strong or relatively weak dollar?

Name:_____**Professor:**_____
Section:_____**Date:**_____

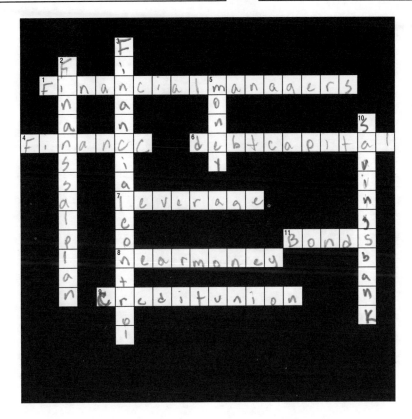

ACROSS

1. Those responsible for developing and implementing the firm's financial plan and for determining the most appropriate sources and uses of funds. (2 words)

4. Planning, obtaining, and managing the company's use of funds to accomplish its objectives most effectively.

6. Funds obtained through borrowing. (2 words)

7. A technique of increasing the rate of return on investment through the use of borrowed funds.

8. Assets that are almost as liquid as cash or checking accounts but cannot be used directly as a medium of exchange. (2 words)

9. A member-owned financial cooperative that pays interest to depositors, offers share draft accounts, and makes short-term loans and some home-mortgage loans. (2 words)

11. Certificates of indebtedness sold to raise long-term funds for corporations or government agencies.

DOWN

2. Document that specifies the funds needed by a firm for a period of time, indicates the timing of inflows and outflows, and indicates the most appropriate sources and uses of funds. (2 words)

3. A process that periodically checks actual revenues, costs, and expenses against the forecasts. (2 words)

5. Anything generally accepted as a means of paying for goods and services.

10. A state-chartered bank with operations similar to those of S&Ls. (2 words)

CHAPTER 15 SOLUTIONS

Analysis of Learning Goals

Learning Goal 15.1

1. d   2. c   3. b   4. d

Learning Goal 15.2

Describe

1.   Money is anything which serves the functions of money---that is, it is anything generally acceptable as a means of payment for goods and services.
2.   "Good" money will be characterized by divisibility, portability, durability, difficulty in counterfeiting, and stability.

Listing

1.   Medium of exchange
2.   Store of value
3.   Unit of account

Learning Goal 15.3

1. True
2. False
3. True
4. True
5. False

Learning Goal 15.4

1.   Firm's require funds for several reasons, including running day-to-day business operations, paying for inventory, making interest payments on loans, paying dividends to stockholders, and purchasing land, facilities, and equipment.

2.   Most financial managers will choose to invest the majority of a firm's excess cash in marketable securities, because the opportunity cost of idle cash is foregone interest income that could have been received if it was invested.

Learning Goal 15.5

1. False
2. False
3. True
4. True

328

Learning Goal 15.6
Listing
1.   Trade credit
2.   Unsecured loans
3.   Secured loans
4.   Selling commercial paper

Describe
1.   Sources of long-term financing include long-term loans that can be repaid over one year or longer, bonds, and equity funds (ownership funds obtained from selling stock in the company, selling company assets, reinvesting company earnings, or from additional contributions by the firm's owners and venture capitalists).

2.   Leverage is a technique of increasing the rate of return on investment through the use of borrowed funds. As long as earnings exceed interest payments on borrowed funds, financial leverage will allow a firm to increase the rate of return on stockholders' investment. However, leverage also works in reverse.

Learning Goal 15.7
1. d   2. a   3. b   4. c   5. d

Learning Goal 15.8
1. True
2. False
3. True
4. True
5. True

Learning Goal 15.9
1. True   2. True   3. True   4. True

Learning Goal 15.10
Many U. S. banks and financial companies earn substantial revenues from outside the United States. Like the United States, most nations have a central banking authority that controls the money supply. Policymakers at these banks often respond to changes in the U.S. financial system by making similar changes in their own systems; these changes can impact countries around the world.

International banks and financial service firms play an important role in global business. They help transfer purchasing power from buyers to sellers, and from lenders to borrowers. They also provide credit to importers and reduce the risks associated with exchange rates. Without a doubt, today, we truly live in a *global* financial community.

Self-Review

True or False

1. T	4. F	7. T	10. F	13. T
2. T	5. T	8. T	11. F	14. T
3. F	6. F	9. T	12. F	

Multiple Choice

1. d	4. e	7. a	10. a	13. d
2. c	5. a	8. d	11. a	14. c
3. b	6. d	9. b	12. e	15. b

Application Exercises

1. a. Company A is leveraged because it has used debt financing (bonds) to raise funds.

    b. Yes, leverage worked for Company A because the company's rate of return to stockholders (the rate of return on investment) due to the use of borrowed funds (the issuing of bonds) is higher than the rate of return to stockholders for Company B. Note:

Company A   **Company B**

rate of return to stockholders = $\dfrac{25,000}{50,000}$ = 50%   rate of return to stockholders = $\dfrac{40,000}{200,000}$ = 20%

    c. Company A will now have a negative return to stockholders (-10%; a loss) because of the $15,000 interest expense which must be paid. This company will have to seek out more funds from somewhere to meet its interest expense. However, Company B will still have a positive return to stockholders of 5%.

    The potential problems with the use of leverage to increase the return on investment include: (1) a lower earnings could result in a loss to stockholders. So, note that leverage makes a good thing better (high earnings produces a high rate of return), but it makes a bad thing worse (low *earnings* can actually produce a *loss* to stockholders). This is why leveraging a company can be risky. (2) The use of debt financing reduces management's flexibility in future decisions because of the fixed interest expense which must be paid.

330

2.	An increase in the supply of money will make credit more readily available, thereby reducing interest rates. Businesses, as well as consumers, will borrow more money at lower rates of interest. These borrowed funds will be spent increasing the demand for goods and services. More goods and services sold will encourage businesses to produce more. More output produced increases employment. More people working, as well as those previously employed but now working overtime or receiving higher wages, increases the nation's income level. More income means even more spending, which will further stimulate the increase in output, employment, and incomes. The process continues, spurring the economy on still further, until something causes people to stop spending as much.

Also note that a decrease in the money supply curtails spending, thereby moderating the inflation experienced when the economy is overheating.

3.	Suppose there is an increase in the exchange rate value of the dollar (the dollar gets stronger; it appreciates). This means that it takes fewer dollars to buy a unit of a foreign currency. Because all products are ultimately priced in their own domestic currency, a stronger dollar means the relative price of foreign imports are cheaper to Americans. Americans will therefore import more when the dollar gets stronger.

On the other hand, a stronger dollar means that it now takes more units of a foreign currency to purchase a single dollar. Therefore, American products will become relatively more expensive to foreigners, and the United States will sell less abroad---the U.S. will export less. Notice that a strong enough dollar in foreign exchange markets will create a trade deficit---imports will exceed exports.

Holding everything else the same, American firms would prefer a weaker dollar because this causes the relative price of American goods and services to be more price competitive (to be relatively cheaper) in international markets. American exporting firms will sell more abroad when the dollar is cheaper (when it depreciates, or gets weaker).

Crossword Puzzle

CHAPTER 15

Chapter 16

The Securities Market

"More than 47 million people own shares in publicly traded corporations; this represents one out of every four U.S. households." (340)

KEY CONCEPTS

Securities	Obligations on the part of their issuers to provide purchasers with an expected or stated return on the funds invested or loaned. (340)
Primary market	A securities market in which securities are first sold to the public. (340)
Investment banker	A financial intermediary who specializes in selling new issues of stocks and bonds for business firms and government agencies. (341)
Secondary markets	Places where previously issued shares of stocks and bonds are traded. (341)
Common stock	The basic form of corporate ownership. (342)
Preferred stock	Stock whose owners receive preference in the payment of dividends; and they have a claim on the firm's assets before any claim by common stockholders. (342)
Secured bond	A bond backed by specific pledges of company assets. (343)
Debentures	Bonds backed only by the reputation of the issuing corporation or government unit. (343)
Institutional investor	An organization that invests its own funds or those it holds in trust for others. (345)
Speculation	The hope of making a large profit on stocks within a short time. (346)

334

Yield	The income received from securities investments; sometimes called the investor's return. (347)
Stock exchange	Where stocks and bonds are bought and sold. (247)
National Association of Securities Dealers Automatic Quotation (NASDAQ)	A nationwide over-the-counter (OTC) network. (350)
Bull	An investor who expects stock prices to rise. (351)
Bear	An investor who expects stock prices to decline. (351)
Price-earnings ratio (P/E) ratio	The current market price divided by the annual earnings per share. (353)
Doe Jones Averages (the Dow)	Average based on market prices of 30 industrial, 20 transportation, and 15 utility stocks that reflect general market activity. (353)
Mutual funds	Financial organizations that pool investment money from purchasers of their securities and use the money to acquire a diversified portfolio of securities. (354)
Program trading	A controversial practice in which computer systems are programmed to buy and sell securities if certain conditions arise. (355)
Insider trading	Illegal securities trading by persons who profit from their access to nonpublic information about a company. (355)

Name:_____Professor:_____

Section:_____Date:_____

ANALYSIS OF LEARNING GOALS

Learning Goal 16.1

Distinguish between primary markets for securities and secondary markets. (340-341)

Multiple Choice

1.   The primary market is:
    a.   where previously issued securities are bought and sold.
    b.   a market in which securities are first sold to the public.
    c.   where stocks, not bonds, are sold.
    d.   A firm may raise funds by issuing stocks, but not bonds.

2.   Which of the following statements is true?
    a.   Stocks are units of ownership in a corporation.
    b.   Bonds do not imply any ownership rights over the assets of the issuer of those bonds.
    c.   An investment banker is a financial intermediary who specializes in selling new issues of stocks and bonds for business firms and government agencies.
    d.   All of the above.

3.   Which of the following statements is true?
    a.   Securities are obligations on the part of their issuers to provide purchasers with an expected or stated return on the funds invested or loaned.
    b.   Stocks and bonds are bought and sold in primary and secondary markets.
    c.   Although a corporation could market its stock or bond issue directly to the public, most large offerings are handled by financial specialists called investment bankers, or underwriters.
    d.   All of the above.

4.   The secondary market:
    a.   is where previously issued shares of stock s and bonds are traded.
    b.   adds liquidity to stocks and bonds because it increases the ease with which these securities can be turned into cash.
    c.   transactions do not effect the gains or losses of the issuing corporation; instead, any gains or losses in the price of a security affects only the current and future owners of these securities.
    d.   All of the above.

Learning Goal 16.2

Compare common stock, preferred stock, and bonds, and explain why investors might prefer each type of security (341-346)

Multiple Choice

1. Common stock:
    a.   is stock whose owners receive preference in the payment of dividends; and they have a claim on the firm's assets before any claim by any other stockholders.
    b.   the basic form of corporate ownership.
    c.   is backed by specific pledges of company assets.
    d.   pays dividends which are guaranteed.

2. Holders of common stock:
    a.   vote on company decisions.
    b.   benefit from company success, but risk the loss of their investment if the company fails.
    c.   are said to have a residual claim to company assets.
    d.   all of the above.

3. Which of the following statements is true?
    a.   Preferred stockholders are paid before common stockholders. and therefor attract more conservative investors.
    b.   Purchasers of common stock expect to receive payments in the form of dividends and/or capital gains resulting from increases in the value of their stock holdings.
    c.   Convertible preferred stock gives stockholders the option of having their preferred stock converted into common stock at a stated price.
    d.   All of the above.

4. Which of the following statements is true?
    a.   Par value is the price at which a stock is currently selling.
    b.   Book vale is determined by subtracting the company's liabilities from its assets, minus the value of any preferred stock.
    c.   The market value of a stock is printed on the stock certificate.
    d.   Preferred stock is the basic form of corporate ownership.

5.   Bonds:
    a.   which are backed only by the reputation of the issuing corporation or government unit are called secured bonds.
    b.   backed by specific pledges of company assets are called debentures.
    c.   which that can be converted into a specified number of shares of common stock are called convertible bonds.
    d.   which represent funds borrowed by the U.S. government are called municipal bonds.

6.   Which of the following statements is true?
    a.   Two factors determine the price of a bond: the degree of risk and its interest rate.
    b.   An institutional investor is an organization that invests its own funds or those it holds in trust for others.
    c.   Institutional investors have become the most important force in today's securities market.
    d.   All of the above.

Learning Goal 16.3
Identify the four basic objectives of investors and the types of securities most likely to accomplish each objective. (346-350)

Listing

List the basic objective of an investor as exemplified by each of the following statements.

Growth 1.   Investors who choose this objective are likely to benefit from stock splits, which typically occur in fast-growing companies like Wal-Mart.

Income 2.   Investors motivated primarily by this goal concentrate on the dividends of prospective companies.

Safety 3.   Investors whose primary objective is this goal are likely to purchase high-quality bonds and preferred stocks.

Speculation 4.   Investors with this objective may act on a corporate rumor or simply purchase high-risk stocks, such as low-priced penny stocks.

Learning Goal 16.4
Explain the process of selling or purchasing a security listed on the organized securities exchanges. (350-352)

Describe

Explain the process of selling or purchasing a security listed on the organized securities exchanges.

Learning Goal 16.5
Describe the information included in stock, bond, and mutual fund quotations. (352-354)

1.   Describe the information included in stock quotations.

2.   Describe the information included in bond quotations.

3.   Describe the information included in mutual fund quotations.

Learning Goal 16.6
Explain the role of mutual funds in the securities field. (354-355)

True or False

T   1.   Many investors who neither have the time nor the knowledge to continually analyze stock market developments may choose another investment option--- mutual funds.

F   2.   Mutual funds are securities markets in which newly issued securities are traded.

T   3.   Investors who buy shares of stock in a mutual fund become part owners of a large number of companies, thereby lessening the individual risk.

F   4.   The percentage of household equity assets held in mutual funds has fallen sharply since 1981.

340

Learning Goal 16.7
Evaluate the major features of state and federal laws designed to protect investors. (351;355)

Describe

Evaluate the major features of state and federal laws designed to protect investors.

True or False

_T_ 1.　Unethical practices typically lead to the passage of laws aimed at restricting such practices in the future.

_F_ 2.　Program trading refers to illegal securities trading by persons who profit from their access to nonpublic information about a company.

_F_ 3.　Insider trading refers to a controversial practice in which computer systems are programmed to buy and sell securities if certain conditions arise.

_T_ 4.　Programmed trading started as a type of portfolio insurance that allowed market players to hedge their bets with automatic buy or sell orders whenever their stock prices reached a certain level.

Name:_____Professor:_____
Section:_____Date:_____

SELF REVIEW

True or False

___T___ 1.   The secondary market is where previously issued securities are bought and sold.

___T___ 2.   In general, the level of risk associated with a bond is reflected in the bond's rating.

___F___ 3.   Stocks and bonds both imply ownership rights.

___F___ 4.   There are two types of bonds: common and preferred.

___T___ 5.   Bondholders are creditors, not owners, of a corporation, not-for-profit organization, or government unit.

___T___ 6.   Bonds have a maturity date, stocks do not.

___T___ 7.   Common stocks are the most risky, but offer investment growth; whereas preferred stocks have limited growth opportunities, but are reasonably safe and offer a steady income.

___T___ 8.   An over-the-counter (OTC) market is an informal method of trading securities through market makers who fill customers' buy and sell orders through computers, by way of teletype, fax machines, and telephones, like the NASDAQ.

___F___ 9.   The price earnings (P/E) ratio equals the current price multiplied by the annual earnings per share

___T___ 10. Dow Jones Averages are a feature of most daily television and radio newscasts and is the report of current stock averages.

___T___ 11. Mutual funds are professionally managed investment companies that own shares in many different companies and allow the investor to purchase their shares of the mutual fund, thereby creating a diversified portfolio.

___T___ 12. Program trading refers to a controversial practice in which computer systems are programmed to buy and sell securities if certain conditions arise.

___T___ 13. Insider trading refers to an illegal securities trading by persons who profit from their access to nonpublic information about a company.

342

Multiple Choice

1.   Which of the following statements is true?
        a.   Long-term debt capital exists in the form of corporate bonds, U.S. government bonds, and municipal bonds.
        b.   Equity capital takes the form of stocks---shares of ownership in the corporation.
        c.   Stocks and bonds are commonly referred to as securities.
        d.   Securities represent obligations on the part of their issuers to provide purchasers with an expected or stated return on the funds invested or loaned.
        e.   .All of the above.

2.   Which of the following statements is true?
        a.   The primary market is where previously issued securities are bought and sold.
        b.   Stocks imply ownership rights, bonds do not.
        c.   A firm may raise funds by issuing either stocks or bonds.
        d.   An investment banker is a financial intermediary who specializes in selling new issues of stocks and bonds for business firms and government agencies.
        e.   All of the above.

3.   Which of the following statements is true?
        a.   Stocks and bonds are bought and sold in primary and secondary markets.
        b.   Although a corporation could market its stock or bond issue directly to the public, most large offerings are handled by financial specialists called investment bankers, or underwriters.
        c.   Secondary market transactions do not effect the gains or losses of the issuing corporation; instead, any gains or losses affects only the current and future owners of those securities.
        d.   An institutional investor is an organization that invests its own funds or those it holds in trust for others.
        e.   All of the above.

4.   Which of the following statements is true?
        a.   Preferred stockholders have voting rights, but they have only a residual claim on the firm's assets.
        b.   Common stockholders receive preference in the payment of dividends and have first claim on the firm's assets after debts have been paid, but usually do not have voting rights.
        c.   Debentures are bonds backed only by the reputation of the issuing corporation or government unit.
        d.   An institutional investor is one who practices "insider trading."
        e.   A callable bond is a bond which can be converted into a specified number of shares of stock.

5.   Yield:
      a.   is the income received from securities investments; sometimes called the investor's return.
      b.   is calculated by multiplying dividends by market price.
      c.   remains the same as the market price and the dividend payment changes.
      d.   is the most important element of a stock for a speculative-minded investor.
      e.   all of the above.

6.   Which of the following is true about securities exchanges?
      a.   A stock exchange is where stocks and bonds are sold.
      b.   The American Stock exchange is the largest and best known of all stock exchanges.
      c.   The New York stock exchange is a smaller organized stock exchange than the American Stock Exchange and handles smaller firms with national following.
      d.   Overseas trading volume of securities is rising more slowly than U.S. trading.
      e.   International, or global, stock exchanges are not yet a reality.

7.   A bear is:
      a.   is an investor who expects stock prices to rise.
      b.   is an investor who expects stock prices to fall.
      c.   is a trained specialist in stock exchanges, most often called a stockbroker.
      d.   what securities dealers are willing to pay for a security.
      e.   a discount brokerage firm.

8.   Which of the following would you *not* find among NYSE stock quotations?
      a.   The highest and lowest trading prices during the past 52 weeks.
      b.   The company's profits.
      c.   The dividend.
      d.   The price-earnings (PE) ratio.
      e.   The stock's highest and lowest prices for that day.

9.   Mutual funds:
      a.   have become very popular as an investment alternative since 1981.
      b.   are financial organizations that pool investment money from purchasers of their securities and use the money to acquire a diversified portfolio of securities.
      c.   are particularly attractive to investors who have neither the time nor the knowledge to continually analyze stock market developments.
      d.   enable individual investors to lower the risk of buying financial instruments.
      e.   all of the above.

344

10.   Which of the following statements is true?
       a.   Insider trading is prohibited by the Securities Exchange Act of 1934.
       b.   A bid price is a price a stock trader is willing to sell a stock for.
       c.   The New York Stock Exchange is a nationwide over-the-counter (OTC) network.
       d.   If a security is "liquid" that means the taxes on its income is relatively low.
       e.   A municipal bond is a debt issue of the U.S. government.

Name:_____Professor:_____

Section:_____Date:_____

<u>APPLICATION EXERCISES</u>

1.   What does the Dow Jones Industrial Average (the Dow) measure? How is the Dow calculated?

2.   What is the relationship between a bond's price and its yield?

Name:_____ **Professor:**_____

Section:_____ **Date:**_____

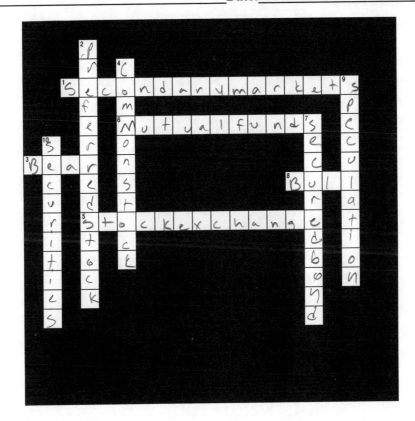

ACROSS

1. Places where previously issued shares of stocks and bonds are traded. (2 words)

3. An investor who expects stock prices to decline.

5. Where stocks and bonds are bought and sold. (2 words)

6. Financial organizations that pool investment money from purchasers of their securities and use the money to acquire a diversified portfolio of securities. (2 words)

8. An investor who expects stock prices to rise.

DOWN

2. Stock whose owners receive preference in the payment of dividends; and they have a claim on the firm's assets before any claim by common stockholders. (2 words)

4. The basic form of corporate ownership. (2 words)

7. A bond backed by specific pledges of company assets. (2 words)

9. The hope of making a large profit on stocks within a short time.

10. Obligations on the part of their issuers to provide purchasers with an expected or stated return on the funds invested or loaned.

CHAPTER 16 SOLUTIONS

Analysis of Learning Goals

Learning Goal 16.1
1. b   2. d   3. d   4. d

Learning Goal 16.2
1. b   2. d   3. d   4. b   5. c   6. d

Learning Goal 16.3
1.   Growth
2.   Income
3.   Safety
4.   Speculation

Learning Goal 16.4
Securities purchases and sales are handled by a trained specialist, called a stockbroker. Once the receives a customer's order, it is conveyed to the stock exchange through a communication terminal. The firm's floor broker executes the sale, and a confirmation is communicated to the broker, who notifies the customer that the transaction has been completed.

Learning Goal 16.5
1.   Information in NYSE stock quotations includes: the 52-week indicator, highest and lowest trading prices during the past 52 weeks, the company's name, stock footnotes, dividend, yield, price-earnings (PE) ratio, projected price-earnings (PPE) ratio, volume, the stock's highest and lowest prices for that day, closing price for that day, and the stock's change in price from the close of the previous trading day.

2.   Bond quotations include maturity date and interest rate, current yield, volume, high, low, and closing price for the day, and a comparison of the closing price with that of the previous day.

3.   Tables of mutual funds list the fund's net asset value (NAV), sale price, and change in the fund's asset value from the previous session.

Learning Goal 16.6
1. True   2. False   3. True   4. False

350

Learning Goal 16.7
Describe
See the Table on page 351.

True or False
1. True   2. False   3. False   4. True

Self-Review

True or False
1. T	4. F	7. T	10. T	13. T
2. T	5. T	8. T	11. T	
3. F	6. T	9. F	12. T	

Multiple Choice
1. e	4. c	7. b	10. a
2. e	5. a	8. b	
3. e	6. a	9. e	

Application Exercises

1.   The Dow measures the general movement of prices of stocks traded on the New York Stock Exchange (NYSE) as a whole.

To compute the Dow, the following 30 big, well known companies' stock prices are added together and then divided by a number slightly less than five. How the number lightly less than five is derived is a long "statistical" story. Nevertheless, these 30 companies are chosen because it is argued that changes in these companies' stock prices are representative of what is happening in the overall stock market.

Alcoa	Goodyear Tire and Rubber
Allied Signal	IBM
American Express	International Paper
AT&T	McDonald's
Bethlehem Steel	Minnesota M&M
Boeing Co.	J. P. Morgon
Caterpillar, Inc.	Philip Morris
Chevron	Proctor & Gamble
Coca-Cola	Sears, Roebuck
Disney	Texaco
Du Pont	Union Carbide
Eastman Kodak	United Carbide
Exxon	United Technologies
General Electric	Westinghouse
General Motors	Woolworth

2.   The relationship between a bond's price and its yield is an inverse one. That is, whatever happens to the price of a bond, its yield will do the opposite. Suppose a $1,000 bond pays an interest rate of 10% or $100 annually. If you paid $1,000 for the bond the yield would be 10% ($100/$1,000). Now suppose the market price increases to $1,100 (possibly because the current market interest rates went down and the 10% guaranteed annual payment associated with this bond now looks very attractive). You sell the bond to someone else This person will now realize that the yield has gone down to 9.09% ($100/$1,100). As the price of a bond goes up, its yield goes down; and vice versa.

352

Crossword Puzzle

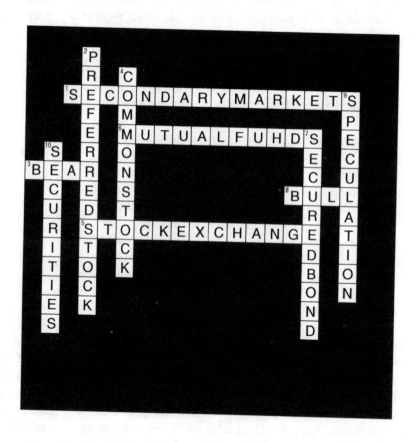

Appendix **A**

Risk Management and Insurance

"...the manager has four methods f dealing with risk: avoiding it, reducing its frequency and/or severity, self-insuring against it, or shifting the risk to insurance companies." (360)

KEY CONCEPTS

Risk	Uncertainty about loss or injury. (360)
Speculative risk	Chance of making either a profit or a loss. (360)
Pure risk	Involves only the chance of risk. (360)
Self-insurance fund	Special fund created by setting aside cash reserves on a periodic basis to be drawn upon only in the event of a financial loss resulting from the assumption of a pure risk. (361)
Insurance	The process by which a firm, for a fee, agrees to pay another firm or individual a sum of money stated in a written contract when a loss occurs. (361)
Insurable interest	The policyholder must stand to suffer loss, financial or otherwise, due to fire, accident, death, or lawsuit. (362)
Insurable risk	The requirements a risk must meet in order for the insurer to provide protection against its occurrence. (362)
Law of large numbers	A probability calculation of the likelihood of the occurrence of peril on which premiums are based. (362)
Mortality table	Used to predict the number of people in each age category who will die in a given year. (362)
Insurance company	Private and a number of public agencies that provide insurance coverage for business firms, not-for-profit organizations, and individuals. (363)

354

Property losses	Financial losses resulting from interruption of business operations or physical damage to property as a result of fires, accidents, theft, or other destructive occurrences. (365)
Liability losses	Financial losses suffered by a business firm or individual should the firm or individual be held responsible for property damage or injuries suffered by others. (365)
Health insurance	Coverage for losses due to sickness or accidents. (366)
Health maintenance organization (HMO)	Prepaid medical expense plan that provides a comprehensive set of health services and benefits to policyholders. (366)
Key executive insurance	Life insurance designed to reimburse the organization for the loss of the services of an important executive and to cover the expense of securing a qualified replacement. (367)

Name:_____**Professor:**_____

Section:_____**Date:**_____

ANALYSIS OF LEARNING GOALS

Learning Goal Appendix A.1
*Explain what is risk and describe the two major types of risk
facing a business organization.* (360)

True or False

__T__ 1.   Risk is the uncertainty about loss or injury.

__F__ 2.   Speculative risk involves only the chance of risk.

__F__ 3.   Pure risk involves the chance of making either a profit or a loss.

__T__ 4.   The two major types of risk are speculative risk and pure risk.

Learning Goal Appendix A.2
Explain how business managers deal with risk. (360-362)

Listing

List the ways in which business managers attempt to deal with risk as described by the following statements.

__Avoiding Risk__ 1.   Although avoiding risk may ensure profitability, it stifles innovation and, as a result, risk-averse companies are rarely leaders in the industry.

__Reducing Risk__ 2.   Although risk cannot be eliminated, many companies develop safety programs to educate workers about potential hazards and the proper methods of performing certain dangerous tasks.

Self-insuring against risk 3. A special fund is created by setting aside cash reserves on a periodic basis to be drawn upon only in the event of a financial loss resulting form the assumption of a pure risk.

shifting risk to an insurance company 4. The process by which a firm, for a fee, agrees to pay another firm or individual a sum of money stated in a written contract when a loss occurs.

Learning Goal Appendix A.3

Describe the three basic principles operating in insurance. (362-363)

True or False

T 1. Three basic principles operate in insurance: the concept of insurable interest, the concept of insurable risks, and the law of large numbers.

F 2. Insurable risk exists when the policyholder must stand to suffer loss, financial or otherwise, due to fire, accident, death, or lawsuit.

F 3. Law of large numbers is used to predict the number of people in each age category who will die in a given year.

F 4. Insurable interest is the requirements a risk must meet in order for the insurer to provide protection against its occurrence

---

Learning Goal Appendix A.4

Describe why insurance premiums differ according to risk. (363)

Describe

Describe why insurance premiums differ according to risk.

Learning Goal Appendix A.5
Identify the different types of public and private insurance companies. (363-365)

Listing
List the different public insurance companies as described by the following statements.

Unemployment Insurance   1.   It assists unemployed workers by providing financial benefits, job counseling, and placement services typically for a period of 26 to 39 weeks.

Worker's Compensation   2.   Guarantees a payment of wages and salaries, medical care cost, and such rehabilitation services as retraining, job placement, and vocational rehabilitation to employees who are injured on the job.

Social Security 3.   This insurance is titled *Old-Age, Survivors, Disability, and Health Insurance (OASDHI)*.

List the private insurance companies as described by the following statements.

Stock Insurance Company   4.   This type of private insurance company is operated for profit.

Mutual Companies 5.   This type of private insurance company is owned by its policyholders.

Learning Goal Appendix A.6
Describe the different types of insurance. (365-367)

Describe
Describe the different types of insurance.

358

Matching

Match the following terms with their descriptions below.

a.   Property losses   d.   Health maintenance organization (HMO)
b.   liability losses   e.   Life insurance
c.   health insurance   f.   Key executive insurance

__F__ 1.   Life insurance designed to reimburse the organization for the loss of the services of an important executive and to cover the expense of securing a qualified replacement.

__D__ 2.   Prepaid medical expense plan that provides a comprehensive set of health services and benefits to policyholders.

__C__ 3.   Coverage for losses due to sickness or accidents.

__B__ 4.   Financial losses suffered by a business firm or individual should the firm or individual be held responsible for property damage or injuries suffered by others.

__A__ 5.   Financial losses resulting from interruption of business operations or physical damage to property as a result of fires, accidents, theft, or other destructive occurrences.

__E__ 6.   This type of insurance deals with the most certain risk of them all.

Learning Goal Appendix A.7
Identify the challenges facing the insurance industry. (367-369)

Describe
Describe the challenges facing the insurance industry.

Name:_____**Professor:**_____
Section:_____**Date:**_____

SELF REVIEW

True or False

___T___ 1.   The two major types of risk are speculative risk and pure risk.

___T___ 2.   Pure risk involves only the chance of risk.

___F___ 3.   Insurance is a special fund created by setting aside cash reserves on a periodic basis to be drawn upon only in the event of a financial loss resulting from the assumption of a pure risk.

___T___ 4.   Insurance companies represent a major source of long-term financing for other businesses.

___T___ 5.   Three basic principles operate in insurance: the concept of insurable interest, the concept of insurable risks, and the law of large numbers.

___T___ 6.   A mortality table is used to predict the number of people in each age category who will die in a given year.

___F___ 7.   Insurance premiums are lower the greater the risk.

___T___ 8.   Insurance companies are private and a number of public agencies that provide insurance coverage for business firms, not-for-profit organizations, and individuals.

___F___ 9.   Unlike the mutual company, the private stock insurance company earns no profit for its owners.

___T___ 10.   Insurance companies, whether stock or mutual companies, have the objective of minimizing the premiums necessary to cover operating expenses and to pay for personal or property losses.

___T___ 11.   Liability losses are financial losses suffered by a business firm or individual should the firm or individual be held responsible for property damage or injuries suffered by others.

___T___ 12.   Cost of health care and the issue of who gets it will likely remain a topic of discussion for some time.

Multiple Choice

1. When a company creates a special fund by setting aside cash reserves on a periodic basis to be drawn upon only in the event of a financial loss resulting from the assumption of a pure risk, then the company is attempting to deal with risk by:
    a.   avoiding risk
    b.   reducing risk
    c.   self-insuring against risk
    d.   shifting risk to an insurance company
    e.   asking for risk.

2. The process by which a firm, for a fee, agrees to pay another firm or individual a sum of money stated in a written contract when a loss occurs is which of the following ways in which a company is attempting to deal with risk?
    a.   avoiding risk
    b.   reducing risk
    c.   self-insuring against risk
    d.   shifting risk to an insurance company
    e.   asking for risk.

3. Law of large numbers indicates:
    a.   that the policyholder must stand to suffer loss, financial or otherwise, due to fire, accident, death, or lawsuit.
    b.   that the requirements a risk must meet in order for the insurer to provide protection against its occurrence.
    *c.   a probability calculation of the likelihood of the occurrence of peril on which premiums are based.
    d.   the number of people in each age category who will die in a given year.
    e.   pure risk does not exist.

4. Workers' compensation:
    a.   assists unemployed workers by providing financial benefits, job counseling, and placement services typically for a period of 26 to 39 weeks.
    b.   guarantees a payment of wages and salaries, medical care cost, and such rehabilitation services as retraining, job placement, and vocational rehabilitation to employees who are injured on the job.
    c.   is titled *Old-Age, Survivors, Disability, and Health Insurance (OASDHI)*.
    d.   is a type of private insurance company operated for profit.
    e.   is a type of private insurance company owned by its policyholders.

5. Social security:
   a. assists unemployed workers by providing financial benefits, job counseling, and placement services typically for a period of 26 to 39 weeks.
   b. guarantees a payment of wages and salaries, medical care cost, and such rehabilitation services as retraining, job placement, and vocational rehabilitation to employees who are injured on the job.
   c. is titled *Old-Age, Survivors, Disability, and Health Insurance (OASDHI)*.
   d. is a type of private insurance company operated for profit.
   e. is a type of private insurance company owned by its policyholders.

6. Financial losses suffered by a business firm or individual should the firm or individual be held responsible for property damage or injuries suffered by others represents:
   a. key executive insurance.
   b. health maintenance organization (HMO).
   c. health insurance.
   d. liability losses.
   e. property losses.

7. Coverage for losses due to sickness or accidents represents:
   a. life insurance.
   b. health maintenance organization (HMO).
   c. health insurance.
   d. liability losses.
   e. property losses.

Name:_____Professor:_____
Section:_____Date:_____

APPLICATION EXERCISES

1.   How could higher health care costs create fewer new full-time positions and more new part-time positions?

Name:_____ **Professor:**_____

Section:_____ **Date:**_____

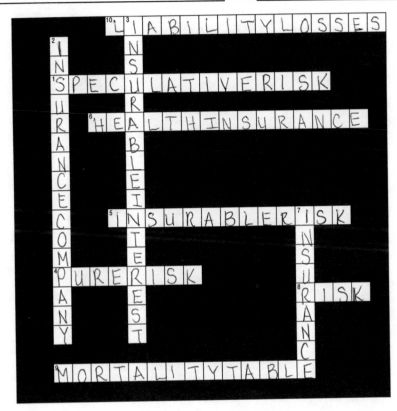

ACROSS

1. Chance of making either a profit or a loss. (2 words)

4. Involves only the chance of risk. (2 words)

5. The requirements a risk must meet in order for the insurer to provide protection against its occurrence. (2 words)

6. Coverage for losses due to sickness or accidents. (2 words)

8. Uncertainty about loss or injury.

9. Used to predict the number of people in each age category who will die in a given year. (2 words)

10. Financial losses suffered by a business firm or individual should the firm or individual be held responsible for property damage or injuries suffered by others. (2 words)

DOWN

2. Private and a number of public agencies that provide insurance coverage for business firms, not-for-profit organizations, and individuals. (2 words)

3. The policyholder must stand to suffer loss, financial or otherwise, due to fire, accident, death, or lawsuit. (2 words)

7. The process by which a firm, for a fee, agrees to pay another firm or individual a sum of money stated in a written contract when a loss occurs.

APPENDIX A: SOLUTIONS

Analysis of Learning Goals

Learning Goal Appendix A.1
1. True   2. False   3. False   4. True

Learning Goal Appendix A.2
1.   Avoiding risk
2.   Reducing risk
3.   Self-insuring against risk
4   Shifting risk to an insurance company

Learning Goal Appendix A.3
1. True   2. False   3. False   4. False

Learning Goal Appendix A.4
Although insurance companies use the law of large numbers to design policies, they often divide individuals and industries into different risk categories and attempt to match premiums to the risk involved, The greater the risk, the greater the premiums.

Learning Goal Appendix A.5
1.   Unemployment insurance
2.   Workers' compensation
3.   Social Security
4.   Stock insurance company
5.   Mutual companies

Learning Goal Appendix A.6
Describe
There are three general types of insurance: (1) property and liability; (2) health; and (3) life insurance.

Matching
1.   f.   Key executive insurance
2.   d   Health maintenance organization (HMO)
3.   c   Health insurance
4.   b   Liability losses
5.   a   Property losses
6.   e   Life insurance

368

Learning Goal Appendix A.7
One of the principal problems facing the insurance industry today is the souring cost of medical care. With the higher costs comes higher premiums and sometimes less coverage. It is a problem which is not likely to go away. Various proposals have been put forth to address the situation. But, because change inevitably alienates someone, it may be difficult to achieve.

Self-Review

True or False

1. T	4. T	7. F	10. T
2. T	5. T	8. T	11. T
3. F	6. T	9. F	12. T

Multiple Choice

1. c	4. b	7. c
2. d	5. c	
3. c	6. d	

Application Exercises

1.   Some people have argued that higher health care costs have already caused businesses to hire more part-time people to fill new positions, as opposed to full=time workers, because health insurance benefits (and the high premiums associated with them) do not have to be provided by employers to part-time workers. Keep in mind, there is some debate surrounding the credibility of some of these statistics. Nevertheless, health care costs are substantial to businesses in the United States.

Crossword Puzzle

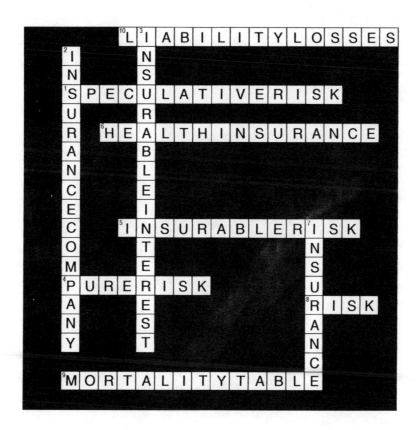

APPENDIX A

Appendix **B**

Fundamentals of Business Law

"One cannot conduct any type of business activity without reference to business law." (372)

KEY CONCEPTS

Law	Consists of the standards set by government and society in the form of either legislation or custom. (372)
Common law	Refers to the body of law arising out of judicial decisions related to the unwritten law the United States inherited fro England. (372)
Statutory law	Includes state and federal constitutions, legislative enactments, treaties of the federal government, and ordinances of local governments. (372)
International law	Refers to the numerous regulations governing international commerce. (372)
Business law	Consists of those aspects of law that most directly influences and regulate the management of various types of business activity. (372)
Judiciary	Is the branch of the government charged with deciding disputes among parties through the application of laws. (372)
Trial courts	A court of general jurisdiction. (372)
Appellate court	A process that allows a higher court to review the case and correct any lower-court error. (373)
Breach of contract	A violation of a valid contract. (374)

Damage	Financial payments made for a loss and related suffering. (374)
Sales law	Involves the sale of goods and services for money or credit. (374)
Negotiable instrument	A form of commercial paper that is transferable among individuals and businesses. (375)
Agency	A legal relationship whereby one party, called a principal, appoints another party, called the agent, to enter into contracts with third parties in the principal's behalf. (376)
Tort	A civil wrong inflicted on other people or their property. (377)
Product liability	Holds businesses liable for negligence in the design, manufacture, sale, and/or use of products. (377)
Bankruptcy	The legal nonpayment of financial obligations. (377)
Trademark	Words, symbols, or other designations used by firms to identify their products. (378)
Patent	Guarantees inventors exclusive rights to their invention for 17 years. (378)
Copyright	Protects written material. (378)

Name:_____Professor:_____

Section:_____Date:_____

ANALYSIS OF LEARNING GOALS

Learning Goal Appendix B.1
*Describe the importance of business law for an organization
and the different types of laws which exist.* (372)

Describe

Describe the importance of business law.

True or False

_____1.   Law consists of the standards set by government and society in the form of either legislation or custom.

_____2.   Common law refers to the body of law arising out of judicial decisions related to the unwritten law the United States inherited fro England.

_____3.   Statutory law includes state and federal constitutions, legislative enactments, treaties of the federal government, and ordinances of local governments.

_____4.   International law refers to the numerous regulations governing international commerce.

Learning Goal Appendix B.2
Identify the nature of business law. (372)

Describe

What is the nature of business law.

Learning Goal Appendix B.3
*Describe the three different types of courts
and their jurisdictions in the American judicial system.* (372-373)

True or False

_____1   The judiciary is the branch of the government charged with deciding disputes among parties through the application of laws.

_____2   Trial courts are a court of general jurisdiction.

_____3   The appellate court is a process that allows a higher court to review the case and correct any lower-court error.

_____4   Administrative agencies exist at all levels of government to decide all types of cases.

Learning Goal Appendix B.4

Identify the 11 major cornerstones of U.S. business law. (373-379)

Matching

Match the 11 following terms and concepts with the appropriate statement found below.

Contract law
Uniform Commercial Code (UCC)
Property law
Law of agency
Bankruptcy law
Tax law

Sales law
Negotiable Instruments
Law of Bailment
Law of torts
Trademarks, patents, and copyrights

_____ 1. Law government legally enforceable contracts.

_____ 2. Involves the sale of goods and services.

_____ 3. Is the basis for commercial law in the United States.

_____ 4. Is a form of commercial paper that is transferable among individuals and businesses.

_____ 5. Law governing the use or right of possession of something.

_____ 6. Is concerned with the surrender of personal property by one person to another when the property is to be returned at a later date.

_____ 7. Law governing a legal relationship whereby one party, called a principal, appoints another party, called the agent, to enter into contracts with third parties in the principal's behalf.

_____ 8. Deals with a civil wrong inflicted on other people or their property.

_____9. Law governing the legal nonpayment of financial obligations.

_____10. Words, symbols, or other designations used by firms to identify their products.

_____11. The branch of law that affects every business, employee, and consumer in the United States.

Name:_____Professor:_____

Section:_____Date:_____

SELF REVIEW

True or False

_____1.   All business decisions must take into account their legal consequences.

_____2.   One cannot conduct any type of business activity without reference to business law.

_____3.   Business law refers to the numerous regulations governing international commerce.

_____4.   Within the federal system, the trial courts are known as U.S. district courts.

_____5.   The feral court system has appellate courts but the states do not.

_____6.   Appeals from general trial courts are heard by an appellate court.

_____7.   Breach of contract is a violation of a valid contract.

_____8.   Damage is financial payments made for a loss and related suffering.

_____9.   Sales law involves the sale of goods and services for money or credit.

_____10.   Agency is a legal relationship whereby one party, called a principal, appoints another party, called the agent, to enter into contracts with third parties in the principal's behalf.

_____11.   Copyright protects written material.

_____12.   A patent guarantees inventors exclusive rights to their invention for 17 years.

Multiple Choice

1. Common law refers to:
    a. the standards set by government and society in the form of either legislation or custom.
    b. the body of law arising out of judicial decisions related to the unwritten law the United States inherited fro England.
    c. state and federal constitutions, legislative enactments, treaties of the federal government, and ordinances of local governments.
    d. the numerous regulations governing international commerce.
    e. all of the above.

2. The type of law which includes state and federal constitutions, legislative enactments, treaties of the federal government, and ordinances of local governments is called:
    a. statutory law.
    b. common law.
    c. international law.
    d. business law.
    e. tort law.

3. Business law consists of:
    a. those aspects of law that most directly influences and regulate the management of various types of business activity.
    b. the standards set by government and society in the form of either legislation or custom.
    c. the body of law arising out of judicial decisions related to the unwritten law the United States inherited fro England.
    d. state and federal constitutions, legislative enactments, treaties of the federal government, and ordinances of local governments.
    e. the numerous regulations governing international commerce.

4. Which of the following statements is true?
    a. Parties not satisfied with a verdict at the state supreme court can appeal to the U.S. Supreme court.
    b. People often represent themselves in small claims court.
    c. The National Labor Relations Board is an example of an administrative agency.
    d. Trial courts are courts of general jurisdiction.
    e. All of the above.

5.   Tort is:
   a.   a civil wrong inflicted on other people or their property.
   b.   a form of commercial paper that is transferable among individuals and businesses.
   c.   legal nonpayment of financial obligations.
   d.   words, symbols, or other designations used by firms to identify their products. (378)
   e.   a guarantee to inventors that no one will infringe upon their exclusive right to their invention for 17 years.

6   Product liability is:
   a.   a form of commercial paper that is transferable among individuals and businesses.
   b.   holds businesses liable for negligence in the design, manufacture, sale, and/or use of products.
   c.   the legal nonpayment of financial obligations.
   d.   a Word, symbol, or other designation used by a firm to identify its products.
   e.   a breach of contract.

7.   A type of property right is:
   a.   tangible property rights.
   b.   intangible property rights.
   c.   real property rights.
   d.   all of the above.
   e.   none of the above.

8.   The four kinds of endorsements described by Article 3 of the UCC include:
   a.   blank endorsements.
   b.   special endorsements.
   c.   qualified endorsements.
   d.   restrictive endorsements.
   e.   all of the above.

Name:_____**Professor:**_____
Section:_____**Date:**_____

APPLICATION EXERCISES

1. Some people argue that we need tort reform in this country to limit the damages awarded in civil suits brought against the business community. These people argue that by doing so, we will all benefit in lower priced products. The critics argue that if tort is reformed (made less potentially costly to businesses who may lose when sued) then this would reduce the incentive for businesses to ensure their products are safe before they sell them. Who is right?

Name:_____Professor:_____

Section:_____Date:_____

CROSSWORD PUZZLE

ACROSS

1. Refers to the numerous regulations governing international commerce. (2 words)

3. Consists of those aspects of law that are most directly influences and regulate the management of various types of business activity. (2 words)

4. A civil wrong inflicted on other people or their property.

5. The legal nonpayment of financial obligations.

9. Words, symbols, or other designations used by firms to identify their products.

11. Consists of the standards set by government and society in the form of either legislation or custom.

DOWN

2. Includes state and federal constitutions, legislative enactments, treaties of the federal government, and ordinances of local governments. (2 words)

6. A process that allows a higher court to review the case and correct any lower-court error. (2 words)

7. Guarantees inventors exclusive rights to their invention for 17 years.

8. Involves the sale of goods and services for money or credit. (2 words)

10. Financial payments made for a loss and related suffering.

APPENDIX B: SOLUTIONS

Analysis of Learning Goals

Learning Goal Appendix B.1
Describe
One cannot conduct any type of business activity without reference to business law. All business decisions must take into account their legal consequences.

True or False
1. True   2. True   3. True   4. True

Learning Goal Appendix B.2
Business law consists of those aspects of law that most directly influences and regulate the management of various types of business activity. Laws differ from state to state and from one industry to another.

Learning Goal Appendix B.3
1. True
2. True
3. True
4. True

Learning Goal Appendix B.4
1.   Contract law
2.   Sales law
3.   Uniform Commercial Code (UCC)
4.   Negotiable Instruments
5.   Property law
6.   Law of Bailment
7.   Law of agency
8.   Law of torts
9.   Bankruptcy law
10.   Trademarks, patents, and copyrights
11.   Tax law

386

Self-Review

True or False

1. T	4. T	7. T	10. T
2. T	5. F	8. T	11. T
3. F	6. T	9. T	12. T

Multiple Choice

1. b	4. e	7. d
2. a	5. a	8. e
3. a	6. b	

Application Exercises

1. This is a controversial issue. There is no right or wrong answer. One must weigh the benefits against the costs for society after examining *all* the available facts. But, still, one will likely observe equally reasonable people disagreeing on this issue.

Crossword Puzzle

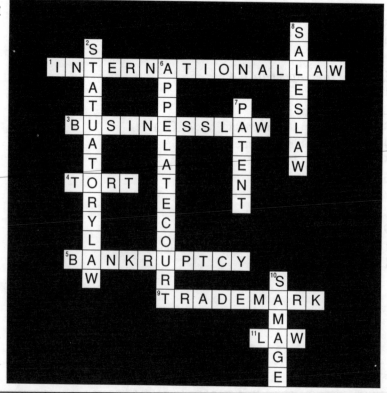